FEET FIRST

Building Momentum Through Collaboration and Connection
in Your Business and Personal Life

GREG GUNTHER and TROY PARSONS

Feet First: building momentum through collaboration and connection in your business and personal life
© Greg Gunther and Troy Parsons 2017

National Library of Australia Cataloguing-in-Publication entry

Creator:	Gunther, Greg, author
Title:	Feet first: building momentum through collaboration and connection in your business and personal life / Greg Gunther ; Troy Parsons.
ISBN:	9780648050490 (paperback)
ISBN:	9780648088806 (ebook)
Subjects:	Mentoring.
	Personal coaching.
	Work-life balance.
	Success.
Other Creators/	
Contributors:	Parsons, Troy, author.

Published by Greg Gunther, Troy Parsons and Ocean Reeve Publishing
www.oceanreeve.com

Ocean
REEVE
PUBLISHING

Contents

'Whatever you need to do and want to do, do it today. There are only so many tomorrows.'

– Anonymous

Preface

Just two ordinary Australian blokes. Two business owners – one of us now a very successful podiatrist globally known as an expert in that field, and the other an equally successful and influential business coach.

We are travelling our own journeys, each one unique. On many counts, our journeys have not been easy but they have been extremely fortunate on others. Looking back now, we came together when we each realised, whether consciously or subconsciously, that we had needs the other would be able to meet. What eventuated was something much more remarkable than we could have ever imagined.

As time enabled our stories to unfold together, we began to open up to each other with complete honesty. Although it was a humbling experience, we both learned to recognise the value of being real. To let down our guards and take off our masks in our personal life and business worlds, at the risk that each of us might think less of the other. For our failures, both small and large, our embarrassments, our mistakes and repeated lessons learnt hard did not merely affect ourselves but those closest to us, in particular our families and friends.

We are all responsible for our own decisions. None of us can blame anything or anyone else for either the good or bad outcomes that result from our actions. Each of us has a choice in everything we do. Yes, there may be contributing factors that sometimes are out of our control, but in the end, the choices we make remain our own.

Whenever we shared our stories with other people, they would ask us to write this book—a book that shares the naked truth of our lives and business ventures from birth to adulthood and beyond. All the choices, mistakes, failures and successes, fears and lessons learned of two ordinary men whose paths finally converged and resulted in incredible personal and professional evolution.

So we both invite you to share our stories from birth to where we are now. To share our hopes and dreams, our fears and failures, our darkest moments and our successes.

Whether you are struggling in business, are extremely successful, or find yourself somewhere in between, we hope you may be able to relate our journeys to your own. Or if you are just interested in reading two life stories depicting how two men's upbringings, experiences, relationships, and life and work choices have moulded them, this book is for you.

Who is this story about? It is about Troy Parsons, a podiatrist who can proudly say he is now an international authority in his field – but not without having made massive mistakes and moving forward to risk new opportunities. It is also about Greg Gunther, a successful international business coach who has also learnt some very hard lessons in life and work, both from his mistakes and his successes.

But we were not always as successful as we are today. Our story has been written as chronological as possible with twists, turns and reflections included as each of our stories unfold. Including hindsight and learnings where relevant along the way.

Hopefully you will gain insight for yourself in some way and relate to some of what we have shared to your own journey, past and future goals. If so, we hope you may benefit from our mistakes, good and not so good choices and journeys, to help you prevent mistakes in your own life and/ or business. Especially in business.

How to grow and travel your own journey while being fully responsible for your own actions, choices and decisions. And uppermost, how to remain real to yourself and others, and that it is OK to not have to 'wear a mask' in business or otherwise no matter how tough things get. And especially, that you must keep moving forward, that it is OK (and in some cases absolutely necessary) to ask for help, even in your darkest hours.

If you don't, perhaps ask yourself this . . . what is the alternative?

Do you wonder why you constantly have to re-learn old lessons in life and business?

Are you struggling in business and find yourself wondering what to do next, or whether you are doing things right?

If so, then read on. This book is for you.

A Note from a Podiatrist – Troy Parsons

I wake up each morning ready to enjoy the day. I am very grateful for what I have and am extremely positive about the future. I have a beautiful family, fantastic friends and a successful business portfolio. I am also proud to be able to say I am an international authority in my field of expertise – podiatry.

None of this was the case nine years ago. In fact it was exactly the opposite. What changed? There was no Lotto win. No corporate promotion. I was fortunate to meet a mentor – Greg Gunther – and through his guidance, I decided to change me. Initially the change mechanism moved slowly. But we worked hard and persevered, change did come.

I had to share my story with you, not as a boast, but because I know too many people are where I was nine years ago . . . and they don't have to be. So in this book, both Greg and I give our own perspectives. We start at the beginning with our own stories of growing up, family, school, our first jobs and relationships and share all the ups and downs of our careers.

All this shows is that we're just two ordinary blokes. But it also shows that no matter where you start, if you plan ahead, plot a course, ask for help and stay true to your goals, then you can achieve your dreams and much more.

If you have been in business, then you will know what rock bottom feels like. I landed there hard one cold Toowoomba morning in July 2008. I was sitting in a coffee shop with a good mate, an exercise physiologist,

Troy Morgan. I was upset and embarrassed, but that was just the caboose in the train wreck that had become my life. An imploding business and an imploded long-term relationship. It was one of those 'it can't get any worse' moments.

During that chat with Troy, I let the façade slip and I found myself telling him how my business was falling apart and my life was a mess.

His response was not what I expected. I looked up to see a big grin on his face!

My first reaction was: 'What the f—k are you smiling at?'

Troy just kept smiling and said: 'Mate, I know somebody who can help you.' He told me he was working with 'a guy' who had experience in the health sector and who 'is awesome'. Troy's parting words that day were – 'The guy's name is Greg Gunther. Here are his details. You should have a talk with him.'

I remember walking away feeling as though hope, like a warm ray of sunshine, had suddenly appeared.

Then began an amazing journey for me, both from a personal and business standpoint. You don't have to flick to the final chapter, I will tell you now – the journey to the point where I am right now has been spectacularly successful for me.

Life is great. It's been nine years since I opened up with Troy that day and I now have an enjoyable life with an array of opportunities I didn't have before. I often use the phrase 'a sliding door' moment. And that was a classic one. If I had not decided to catch up for a chat, been too busy at work, had never met Greg Gunther – I really do shudder to think.

To understand my journey, and hopefully to gain something out of it for yourself, I have to start at the start. I am where I am now not because I am somehow special, lucky or brilliant. I was just a typical small business owner who was working too hard at a business that wasn't doing as well as it should. And my personal life could have been a lot better too at the time. I was drinking too much, smoking too much and not exercising enough. But I now have a breadth of opportunity that I'd never imagined having before.

If you can identify with any of this, then read on, because this book will improve your life, and quite possibly save your business from failing. Or even better, help you grow it to heights you would never have imagined possible. And you might discover your own 'why'. Why you do what you do? My 'why' is to realise my potential. And what does that allow me to do? It allows me to help so many other people realise their own potential. Starting with my family.

A Note from a Coach – Greg Gunther

When I was asked what the purpose and key points of this book should be summarised as, my response was simple. This book is the story of two ordinary blokes sharing their own experiences and how one honest cry for help brought the two of them together to create something really special.

It explains the events, outcomes and lessons of two men who have experienced many highs and lows in both life and business. It also explains how we have learned to endure and learn, and take the lessons from every valuable experience along the way.

Many of us have experienced the truth that it is often darkest just before the dawn. It is difficult, if not impossible, to see our way forward when we are in those dark hours, but there is always a way through. Then there is the fear of failure – something that is in all of us at some point of our lives. My own journey has shown me that there is no such thing as failure. Failures are only lessons waiting to be learned.

We all get to choose our reaction to any circumstances presented to us. In my life there have been many times where I could have reacted differently and seen different results. In my early thirties, I had a business failure and lost absolutely everything. I saw myself as a total failure and I thought my life was over. I had failed myself, my wife and my family. I'd always strived to make my parents proud, but now I'd let them down. I felt even worse because my father lost money due to one of my failures.

Troy and I both had to learn the importance of humility and letting go of our egos. Years ago when Troy called me up and shared some of his story, I saw myself in him, especially from my own years in the corporate world when my ambition and ego got in my way. Now I've learned the importance of laughing at myself and not becoming too attached to particular outcomes.

I also now believe the Universe will provide what you need when you need it. I used to be very goal-driven, focussed on tight objectives while I strove to succeed in the corporate world. And you can create carnage along the way if you aren't open to receiving what the Universe sends. And that was my story. I was too blocked to see the messages.

Then I lost everything. But looking back on that time much later, this difficult period in my life was actually a blessing. It taught me lessons and gave me a gift. Who would have thought failure was a gift and that it would make me stronger?

What lessons did that experience teach me? Now I know that when I hit a wall, there is always another way to get through to my goal. I know that life doesn't have to be hard but sometimes we make it so. We might feel powerless, but actually we are in control of our own destinies. Armed with these insights, I can now help others. I can help them see that we need to start our own journeys towards our dreams, all the while learning from the messages we are sent.

And my gift for being able to see in others what they can't see in themselves enables me to guide them along life's paths. That is my purpose in life, my 'why'—to help others create a more enjoyable life using my skills in business.

This book offers something for every business owner, and every reader will be able to relate to and 'take home' different insights. It describes elements that each of us as business owners have or may have had, including fears that often stop us from doing great things. I am proud to say I have no fear anymore, even after I've experienced massive failures from taking action. Hopefully after reading this book, you too will be more confident in yourself, more willing to take calculated risks and able to reach success.

I have also learnt that if we react to difficulties in a positive rather than a negative way, we can turn our failures into opportunities. True, there are no guarantees in life. What we try may not work, but if we learn lessons from our failures and have the confidence to try something else and see what comes up—and then make another choice, then another—we will continue to move forward.

Life has been a great teacher for me, although many a time I played the victim and asked, 'Why me?' Now I that have reached the halfway point in my life, I can reflect with a certain amount of wisdom and identify the times in my life when I learned my greatest lessons.

Indeed, it has been an incredible journey of many highs and lows, all of which have shaped me into who I am. Now I live a life of purpose, helping others by drawing upon my valuable lessons learnt after three decades of self-employment and building businesses.

But the really cool thing is I get to work alongside great people like Troy Parsons. When I met Troy, there was a 'mirror moment'. Here was a young man in a lot of pain, emotionally and financially. As he poured out his struggles in both his personal and business worlds, I could identify with every ache he felt. I knew what it was like to be lauded and envied by one's peers. I also knew how it felt for the earth to one day just disappear out from under you, and you fall into a deep, dark crevasse of failure, debt, depression and doubt. Having been there myself, I could physically feel his pain. We spoke for an hour and a half—well, he spoke and I listened.

And the more I listened, the more I knew I could help. Despite his gloomy disposition, he convinced me that he wanted to change, to be a better person, to deserve a better life. He was a man whose pride had forced him to build a wall around his emotions. Yet that afternoon the wall came crumbling down and he poured out his problems to a complete stranger. In that moment, I decided to help. What followed was one of the most rewarding journeys of my life.

Troy's story isn't unique. Too many people live every day suffocating under a weighty blanket of failure. But there is no magic wand. The business owner must not only agree to change but be committed to change and actually work hard on that change. Crucially, the shift must come from the business owner. Your business and your struggles and successes are a reflection of who you are. So if you want change, you have to change. And many people who seek my advice are not willing to make that change, so I step away, because to do otherwise would be a waste my time and their money. In Troy Parsons, I immediately saw someone who knew he was in trouble and had a real commitment to improve himself and therefore his podiatry business.

Now, I know very little about podiatry, but I know a great deal about the formulas that make businesses work. I know a lot about the processes and cultures that get businesses into trouble and the processes and cultures that will get those same businesses heading in the right direction. I am a business coach, a mentor. I take people like Troy by the hand and guide them and their business from whatever predicament they are in back to solid ground and to success.

There is a saying I love which explains well the connection that Troy and I have . . .

'When the student is ready the teacher appears.'
– Mabel Collins,
Fellow of the Theosophical Society,
circa 1885

The question is, are you ready?

If so, I invite you to read on and share our journeys through life, pain and victory. While you journey along with us, ask yourself which one of us was really the student and which was the teacher.

'Wisdom is looking back on your life and realising that every single event, person, place and idea was part of the perfected experience you needed to build your dream. Not one was a mistake.'

– Dr John F. Demartini

JUST TWO ORDINARY BLOKES

Just Two Ordinary Blokes

'The present is never our goal:
the past and present are our means: the future alone is our goal. Thus, we
never live but we hope to live; and always hope to be happy, it is inevitable
that we will never be so.'
Blaise Pascal, French mathematician and philosopher

'There comes a special moment in everyone's life, a moment for which that
person was born. That special opportunity, when he seizes it will fulfil his
mission – a mission for which he is uniquely qualified. In that moment, he
finds his greatness. It is his finest hour.' Winston Churchill

A Podiatrist is Born

I will start right at the start … because it shows there is nothing excep-
tional about my life growing up. My mum and step-dad loved me. But
they weren't rich. They worked hard and made sure I had an excellent
education. We were a classic working-class family. I have no doubt
hundreds of thousands of Australians could identify with my journey.
The faces and places may be different, but sections of the path travelled
will look familiar. It just shows that wherever we start from, whatever the
path, we can choose and change the destination.

I came into this world on November 2, 1973, at Southport Hospital, on the beautiful Gold Coast of Queensland, Australia. But like so many of us, I didn't come into a particularly happy home. By the time I was three, my mother and father had separated. Mum (Cheryl), myself and my younger brother (Chris) lived for a few years in the Kingscliff area of northern NSW. By the time I was six, Mum had remarried. Her second husband, Bob Parsons, is the only real father I have known. A champion bloke.

By this stage we had moved back to the Gold Coast and I was in Year 1 at Ashmore State Primary School. Through my story, I will regularly pay tribute to my mother. She is a great person. I have faint memories of her being a single mum – before Bob came along – and working hard to support her family. Mum's parents, Nana and Pa, would also help out a lot back then.

When Bob did come along, financially we were better off and we all felt more secure. When Mum and he were first together, he owned a trucking company. He also had been married previously, and from what I have gleaned, as a result of the divorce and a corrupt business partner, he lost the trucking business. From there he sold real estate on the Gold Coast and then drove taxis. Originally he started out as an optical technician. Although Bob was my step-father, he quickly became our 'Dad' and we had no problem calling him that.

I was at Ashmore Primary School for Years 1 and 2. That time on the Gold Coast was a very happy period. In fact my entire childhood with Mum and Dad was very happy. Here's one memorable moment that's three-parts happy, one-part outrageously embarrassing. It was my first day of Grade 1 and the local newspaper – The Gold Coast Bulletin – wanted take a 'school's back' type of photo to print on the front page.

So the photographer and a teacher selected me and about three other boys, and there we were, standing proudly in our first school uniform. The other boys in the photo were looking cool in their joggers and socks, while I was standing for all the world to see with my socks pulled up to my knees and wearing sandals! Now, that sort of shit is really hard to get over!

My overarching memory of that time is happiness. I think Mum was very unhappy during her first marriage. And then she was by herself. Mum is an incredibly special, beautiful lady and it was wonderful for her to find someone who loved her and took on her two boys as his own. Mum had various part-time jobs. One was at the Carrara Markets, selling stuff that I can't remember. Nana helped her and so we would spend the day with my grandfather, Pa.

We would show up and Mum would leave and Pa would go, 'Right-o, boys, bedtime.' He would put Chris and I to bed at about two o'clock in the afternoon. We would say, 'But, Pa, we're not tired.' The reply was always the same – 'You are going to bed.' That was Babysitting 101 according to Pa.

Although this was a happy time, that doesn't mean there wasn't any discipline. Dad made sure we knew right from wrong. Chris and I had our mouths washed out with soapy water on more than one occasion and there was also the 'Wooden Spoon'. The latter had 'Troy' written on one side and 'Chris' on the other. I'm not sure which side was used more, but I do recall the spoon having to be replaced on many occasions because it was broken on one of our backsides.

Around 1980 when I was seven years old, we moved to Brisbane. My parents had decided to buy a news agency – the Bardon News – which was on McGregor Terrace, Bardon. Whenever I drive past that spot, I can still pinpoint where the shop used to be. We moved into a house at The Gap, and Chris and I went to school at Payne Road State School. I believe Mum and Dad bought the news agency because they wanted autonomy, a bit of control. They were both working for people, and Dad especially wanted to get back to having his own business. News agencies were then good businesses but required long hours and a lot of hard work.

Mum and Dad owned the Bardon News for two and a half years. It was a solid business and they were both worked incredibly hard. They certainly showed me what hard work is and I know I cannot ever whinge about what I do because I have never worked as hard as they did. Dad would get up every morning at 2am to 'throw papers', then got home at

5am to get changed, have something to eat and get back to work. That was every morning – just two days off a year, Good Friday and Christmas Day. Mum worked just as hard. As soon as we went to school, she was in the news agency and then wouldn't get home until late.

This of course meant a bit of 'free' time for Chris and I. We walked home from school but we were not trusted to be inside the house by ourselves at that age. The treat each day was an ice block that was left in the freezer for us in the outdoor laundry. And sometimes we hung out with an older girl who was our next door neighbour. She sometimes let us come over to her place. Too often we just got bored and started breaking stuff. We were just two typical energetic yet bored kids.

So what could we do with all that excess energy? Well, we rode our bikes or just ran around. There was a nearby creek that used to flood pretty easily. We would jump on our boogie boards and ride the flood water underneath a little bridge through the pipe and out the other side. What the hell were we thinking? I recall Chris emerging from the water on one occasion covered in leeches and screaming his head off. He ran home, but by the time he got there, all the leeches had dropped off. That's just one example of the memories we made creating our own adventures.

I remember Chris and I walking home from school one day, and Dad's mum, Grandma, was down from Redcliffe looking after us. We were about to cross Payne Road, which was quite busy. I told Chris, 'Right, go!' and we both started to run across the road. At the last second, I realised a car was coming and I stopped. But Chris didn't, and the car – a police car – just clipped him. He was fine except for a tire mark on his leg after being hit, but, oh my God, Grandma was furious.

Unfortunately there was a series of similar misadventures around that time including Chris and I, and Chris always seemed to be the one getting hurt (the joys of being the younger brother). Again, we weren't bad kids, just energetic and with too much time on our hands. We weren't allowed inside the house until Mum came home so we roamed around and found our own fun outside. But it did cause Dad on one occasion to call in a favour from his mate, who was a police sergeant. We were both marched down to the police station where we were read 'the riot act'.

Chris and I did a lot together. We are really good mates now, but back then I was probably the stereotypical older brother – a bit of an arse. I used to stand over him and knock him around, but Chris was always quick at coming back with a smart reply. He would stir the hell out of me and so I'd react.

After a few years at the news agency, Mum and Dad decided to return to the Gold Coast. I think they were tiring of the long hours and they also both really liked the Coast. By this time I was eleven years old and in Year 6. We moved into a really nice house in Mermaid Waters and Chris and I went to Miami State School. This was our third school in five years, but we didn't know any different. Change was something we thought was normal. In hindsight this was probably a good thing as it taught us to cope well with change and meet new people from a young age.

We quickly grew into typical Gold Coast kids. We didn't wear shoes much and were always at the beach, never at home. Out on our BMX bikes, or just exploring.

That was a really fun period of our lives, but we were soon on the move again. I recall getting ready to go to high school, so I was turning thirteen, and Mum and Dad were keen on me going to The Southport School (TSS), a prestigious private school on the Gold Coast. My parents were not too happy with 'the crowd' that Chris and I hung around with. We weren't getting into really bad stuff, but the potential was there for it to become 'bad'.

So up to Brisbane we went. Mum and Dad wanted to buy another news agency and found one at East Brisbane. We lived with Grandma at Redcliffe for a while because they hadn't found a house to buy yet. Soon after, we were driving through Brisbane and came across Churchie – the Anglican Church Grammar School – which was another prestigious private school. Dad liked the look of it and so I was enrolled there. I was lucky to get accepted. It was quite a trek from Redcliffe, though. Dad would drop me at the train station at 6.30am and I would go from

Shorncliffe down to Brisbane's CBD, jump on a bus to East Brisbane and walk the final leg to school to arrive at 8.15am. So I spent a large part of Grade 8 commuting 30kms each way to and from school in Brisbane. But looking back, it was worth the long trek to school each day.

What an eye-opener that year was! By this stage I had already been to a number of schools but nothing like this. Not only was the school massive, but all the boys seemed so much older and more mature than me. There were guys with hairy legs and beards in Grade 8 and it was my first experience with boarders from Longreach and remote places like that. They seemed like men. It was quite a culture shock.

The private school fees placed Mum and Dad under significant financial stress, but they wanted to give us the best opportunity they could. I can never thank them enough for the sacrifice they made to get us ahead in life. I look back at how hard they worked and it almost broke them. I have massive respect for the sacrifices they made. It was such a gift.

The kids we went to school with came from totally different backgrounds. Very fortunate backgrounds. It showed me what else was actually out there. I saw a lot of diversity, wealth, success, ambition and also envy observing my fellow students who came from wealthier classes.

After I had been at Churchie for six months or so, my parents finally found a house to buy just around the corner from the school. That meant just a five-minute walk for me. They also bought a news agency in Lytton Road – Lytton Road News. Following our relocation to East Brisbane, Chris moved to Coorparoo State school which was a short bus ride away. He was two years below me in Grade 6. While we were living at Redcliffe, Chris went to primary school at nearby Clontarf. It was a local State school, and I recall he was named captain of the soccer team as he was the only one with boots. Although it was rather a low socio-economic school, he coped well in all respects.

Tasting Independence and Self-Discipline

Although Mum and Dad worked strenuously to put Chris and me through private schools, we did not feel an immense pressure to do well because of this. To be honest, yes, they wanted the best for us, but they also wanted us to be happy. They wanted to give us the best opportunities and because they were so busy and so tired, it was really up to us. They worked themselves into the ground, so unfortunately although they wanted us to do well, they were far too busy and exhausted to really watch how we were doing.

Chris and I started to help out by getting up early to throw the papers. Every Friday and Saturday night we would go to sleep and think, 'Oh no, I have to get up tomorrow at 2am and throw papers.' There were good times, but generally, I hated it. We earned $25 a week. The stacks of papers would be delivered to the shop before we arrived and we would have to bring them in, roll them with a special machine (first with paper and in later years, plastic), stack the car and then head out to deliver the papers.

We were expected to do it, but if you'd given me a choice at the time, I would have taken the full night's sleep instead. Yet the experience taught us a lot and we were obviously a big help to Dad (most of the time). Elements of the job were fun for kids, though, so from that I learned about compromise. Some of those paybacks included being able to grab lollies and snacks before starting work and enjoying free magazines and comics from the shop.

Still, none of us were morning people. So we did the best we could to make it fun. We drove around the paper run in a tiny 'Mini Moke' vehicle, tossing the papers out the window as we went. We had all the papers stacked up around us, in piles as high as we were tall. The 'Moke' was a manual and Dad would change gears with one hand and throw papers with the other. Chris and I sat in the back and were in charge of throwing *The Australian* or *The Sunday Sun* – depending on which day it was.

Considering all that was going on in the Moke, there was the potential for disaster, but only a few mishaps ever befell us. Like the morning when Dad was in a fouler mood than normal and took a sharp turn down a driveway. I looked back and – no Chris!

'Hey, Dad!' I yelled.

'WHAT?' came the sharp reply.

'We've lost Chris!' I said, laughing.

He had fallen out the back. Fortunately there was no harm done.

It seems like an easy job, throwing papers. But it was stressful. Obviously you had to throw the right paper into the right yard, but not only that, certain papers had to go under the fence, over the fence or onto a driveway, all while going 40-60km per hour. And Dad would be continually yelling out, 'Did you get it under the gate?' Of course you would always reply 'Yes'. Because if you missed your target, Dad would go off, hit the brakes and reverse back.

So yes, it was stressful and there was a lot of pressure. But we had great throwing arms. We would finish about 4.30am, have an hour or two of sleep and then get ready for Saturday sports. That was just our life. In the afternoons after school we would go to the shop and do bits and pieces of work there and I also delivered papers to the local bowls club. While other boys went off rowing or whatever, we worked. But, again, it showed us the value of hard work and gave us ideas about what we wanted out of life.

So Mum and Dad instilled discipline and a strong work ethic in us from a young age. I have had a job since I was twelve and Chris has had a job since he was ten. And that is the way it was. Moreover through all of this, there was the awareness of how hard Mum and Dad worked to deal with the financial stress incurred by private school tuition. In the end, that strong work ethic became ingrained in the core of who we were as men and gave us the tenacity to endure the storms life would send our way.

Reflecting

Reflecting on my years at Churchie, it was a positive experience overall. In fact I would love to send my son there. But when I see my wife with our son, I realise that although my parents worked so hard for Chris and I to have to have the best possible life, in doing so they were 'never there'. They were always working.

So, although they were leading by example, there was not a lot of pressure, encouragement or support to do well. I would have loved for them to have verbally given more direction or expectations. To have said: 'Hey, listen, we think you should be doing X, Y and Z.' I probably would have liked to have been driven more. I don't mind a bit of pressure.

There is no doubt that many of the students at Churchie were very driven. I distinctly remember a couple of blokes in my class having maturity beyond their years. Because of their upbringing, they were wise at a young age. I recall one of those guys saying, 'Quite frankly, I am just here to get a TE score to get to uni. I get to uni and get a job and then I am going to learn.' And I remember thinking, 'What did he just say?' That style of thinking was so foreign to me.

There was another bloke. He was the school vice-captain – the first in everything, reasonably smart.

During class one day, he said to the teacher, 'Look, I am just under so much pressure. I really don't think I have got enough time to do everything I need to do.'

And here was me thinking, 'I don't have any pressure. I am just doing the best I can. I am just happy to be here. What's for lunch?'

So, in some ways, yes, I would have liked to have been pushed more by my parents. But in others I am so glad that I did not have the weight of expectation that burdened some of my classmates.

Deciding Next Steps

So I was nearing the end of Year 12 in high school and it was becoming apparent that I wasn't going to get the grades I had hoped for to get into a university. The teachers would provide you with a ballpark of what you could expect and I was meant to be on track for a Tertiary Entrance (TE) score of 940 or 945 which would have had me covered for whatever I wanted to do at uni. Those were the days of TE scores, with the highest being 990. Unfortunately I didn't do as well in some of the subjects as I had hoped and ended up with a very average TE score of only 860. I felt like an absolute failure. To say I was disappointed in myself is an understatement. I was gutted.

I set about exploring all of my options, feeling quite sick about it. Initially, I thought I wanted to do law but I had changed my mind after working as a legal aid. It wasn't for me. Then I was keen to look at health. With my grades, I would have been happy just getting into a science major, but even that wasn't achievable with my poor results.

However, I have to admit that my score was a correct indication of my academic efforts in Years 11 and 12. While I did a reasonable amount of homework and study, I wasn't efficient. I worked hard, yet I focussed on the wrong things, allowing stress to affect my grades. I was also more interested in memorising content rather than understanding the process of how and why things work. That's where I fell down.

But the factor that impacted my performance more than any other was a lack of direction. I did not have a career path in mind. I'd visit the guidance counsellor, but I had no idea of what I wanted to do and neither did he. My parents also couldn't supply the answer. Mum and Dad were just so excited that we were going to university. Neither of them had that opportunity and they wanted us to have that chance. So it didn't matter what we were going to study at university. For them, and for me, the fact that I was going to uni at all was enough.

It was different for my mates. They knew that they were going to into medicine or engineering from Grade 8. Again, looking back, there was a lot to be learned from their mindset. One of my mates had a brother who left in Grade 10 to become a carpenter. I remember thinking, 'What a waste! Carpentry!' That was my mindset at the time – 'You have to go to uni.' But by the time I did get to uni, that carpenter already had his first house!

I decided simply to do the best I could. I found out I could go to night school and do two subjects to increase my TE score. So that is what I did. It was time to join the real world and take responsibility for my future. I realised I'd had a setback, but I had to keep moving forward.

A Coach Is Born

Starting right at the beginning, I was born in Naracoorte, South Australia, on 1 April 1959 as the oldest child of three. Straightaway my birthdate created a standard that I have been ragged about all through my life, so I am very thankful it was after midday when I met the world, and the world met me. Officially named Gregory, I was always Greg to everyone except Dad, especially when I was in trouble. Dad always maintained 'what was right' so I was always Gregory in his eyes. I was to learn later the pressure of living up to all of Dad's expectations for me.

Both Mum (Yvonne) and Dad (Barry) came from farming backgrounds. Dad's family had owned a large sheep property at a place called Hawker in the Flinders Ranges in central South Australia. However by the time Dad was fourteen, the property had failed financially and he was literally out on the road droving sheep. In a way, experience with failed business enterprises is in my DNA.

Mum's family has deep roots in Naracoorte. She was born there, went to primary school there and then went off to boarding school in Adelaide. After Mum and Dad married, they annexed 900 acres off Mum's father's property. And that's where they began raising a family. I am the oldest of three. Next is my sister, Kerri, and then my brother, Craig.

By the time I was five in 1964, we were saying goodbye to Naracoorte and the dairy farm. Nine hundred acres just wasn't viable and Mum and Dad decided to sell up and follow members of his family who had already moved north to Queensland. When a farm fails, there are always heartaches and recriminations. For Mum and Dad this was heightened by the fact that they were selling off a slice of ancestral land. That decision caused a rift between Dad and his in-laws. For Mum, that move was also hard as it meant leaving home and her family.

We moved to Toowoomba and for a few years Dad worked for the Australian Wheat Board. The family also made supplementary income renovating houses. Dad had a family friend in real estate in Toowoomba. They bought bargain residential properties – the classic fixer-uppers. Our weekends were often spent painting and landscaping. I can recall the whole family being involved in several make-overs.

However Dad's plan was always to go back to the land. He was a farmer. Fortunately at this time – the mid-1960s – the federal government was encouraging people to become farmers. Large tracts of government leasehold land were made available to prospective farmers who would draw lots for this land. Dad fitted the eligibility criteria and was successful in drawing a block at a place called Hannaford.

The property was about 3600 acres (1450 hectares) of undeveloped, uncleared land. It had been carved off a neighbour's block that he'd been leasing, and of course initially he resented us coming in and 'taking' his land. But over time those feelings thawed and the two families became good friends. At that stage the land needed a lot of work. It was totally unproductive. Sections needed to be cleared. Fences had to be built. We started from scratch.

It was also very basic living. Initially 'home' was a caravan. I have no doubt it was tough for Mum and Dad to make do in a tiny van. We three kids would sleep outside under a lean-to. Mum cooked on a campfire. There was no electricity. But we kids loved it. We had a ball – three young kids running around having fun, living out under the stars. Although it was basic, we survived and I am not sorry for that experience. It helped build my resilience and taught me to take responsibility.

Looking back, it is Mum whom I feel most sorry for. We had just moved into a new home in Toowoomba when Dad drew the block and was randomly assigned that plot of land. The house in Toowoomba though was a new brick home, quite modern for the time, and we all felt settled there. It would have been traumatic for Mum to go from that lovely new home to living in a caravan in the middle of the bush.

When we moved to the farm at Hannaford, I would have been in Grade 2 – seven years old – at the Toowoomba North State School. I remember that was the time of the currency change in 1966. Classes were of about thirty children and I recall using slates and chalk. Things were a little different at Hannaford. It was a one-teacher school and there were only four students in my class.

We lived in the caravan first while our machinery shed was being built with one end of it closed off for us to live in. We lived in that shed for a couple of years before our house construction commenced. Unfortunately this didn't go smoothly either, adding to all the other difficulties at the time. The builder ended up going broke while the house was being built so that stalled the construction for some time. That led to a difficult situation between Dad and the builder that all blew up on a day I will never forget.

I was around nine years old at the time. Dad locked us kids in the shed, doing what he could to protect us when the builder came by and started attacking his car with an axe! We never saw that man again. In the end Dad got a private person to finish the house. He was a lovely Hungarian man who became good friends with the family. So we were promoted once again to better living conditions. This time from a shed to a house.

Dad was a sheep farmer. He always liked sheep. So as he gradually cleared the land, it was sheep that were introduced first. Then a few cows and eventually some crops – oats and then wheat. But it was tough going. I believe I have a good work ethic and that is where it was forged. As a youngster all of our out-of-school hours and weekends were spent improving the property – stick-picking (clearing the land of logs and bushes before planting could start) and fencing.

The bulldozers would come in and knock the trees over so they would eventually die. They were then pushed into windrows (piles of timber). It was our job to walk between the windrows and create piles of sticks which were eventually burnt. This was back-breaking, laborious, slow and boring work, but it gave us a lot of time to think. I hated stick-picking. At only seven or eight years old, I joined the rest of the family in working long hours, sun-up to sun-down.

The remoteness of living out on the farm was just accepted as it was. I recall we had no telephone for many years so we had to travel five miles to the nearest phone line to contact the outside world. Some of the timber we felled was used for telephone poles which are probably still there today. When we did eventually have a telephone, we shared a party line with six other families so we had to take turns to make calls.

Money was tight. Dad left the wheat board job when we moved to the property. So it was a hand-to-mouth existence. I have plenty of memories of Mum and Dad arguing about how we had no money to do things. All the money was going into the property. And Dad must have borrowed money, so there were repayments to make as well. Dad stressed a lot about money and every day was a struggle. I don't remember Dad ever being relaxed. He always seemed to be struggling, worrying and working hard. Unbeknownst to me at the time, my 'outside in' view of his struggles and how he managed to get through it all would become a key influence on my own adult life, and that in the lives of others, in many ways.

So why break your back on the land when we could have had a comfortable life back in Toowoomba? The attraction for my father was the legacy of being a property owner. It was what his father did and his own siblings did. Dad, I believe, was driven by resentment as he the need to prove something to his father. A lot of what we were doing was creating a model farm. It was as if he had to stick it up his father's nose. His father had failed on the land and Dad had to prove that he could do better.

It took about five years before the Hannaford property actually started producing a cash flow, initially from wool. But as soon as we started to produce our own wool, wool prices tumbled, adding to the struggle. I remember my dad always complaining about what he had to pay the shearers. There was nothing left over for us.

Mum and Dad were on that Hannaford property several years before they built a house. After a couple of years we moved out of the caravan and into a room built on the end of the machinery shed. All we had for walls were curtains hanging by a piece of wire.

Mum was a worker. She was out working with us all day and then she would return to the shed and prepare the meals. She worked beside Dad as a labourer, kept the house, did all the laundry and looked after us kids. We had no TV so the entertainment was the radio and whatever else we could find to keep ourselves busy in play. I recall family moments at lunchtime, all sitting down together while listening to *Blue Hills* on ABC radio – a serial that ran every day. It's amazing what stays in your memory after such a long time.

We were also pretty isolated – about 80km from Tara, which was a town of less than a thousand people. It was a three-hour drive to

Toowoomba. We did our grocery shopping there – a once a month affair. Whenever Mum did go to town to shop, she would always bring home a comic and a packet of chewies for me. I used to like Superman; he was my favourite because he was a superhero who saved everyone.

Maybe I liked Superman because I looked up to my Dad and considered him the best farmer, the best everything, and he stood up for what he believed in. He was Superman in his own right. While others might not have agreed, he just wanted to be the best. And to me, he was.

Nevertheless, Dad was a strict father. Not abusive, just very strict, and he had a bad temper. He certainly wielded the stick on us. There was always a beating, always a stick, a belt or something like that for both of us boys, but never my sister as far as I can remember. Dad always had a soft spot for her and in my memory she was 'the favourite'. Perhaps this was natural for him to protect his daughter whereas the boys got the tougher rein.

I can remember Mum was always to the side when this was happening. I suspect she didn't like it, but she never tried to stop him. The only thing I can remember about Mum in relation to discipline was the old 'wait until I tell your father' line. I would get a belting or a berating if I didn't do something properly or put something back where it belonged.

Dad was fanatical about the last person using something always putting it back where it belonged. He liked order. I can't remember beltings over schoolwork or anything like that. It was always something to do with something I had done. Like my brother and I fighting, that would lead to a belting. The ridiculous thing is that the harsh discipline was all about Dad wanting the best for us and that was the only way he thought he could make that happen. Unfortunately I only realised this late in his life – literally when he was on his deathbed. I will share more about this lesson later.

Leaving the Nest

In 1972 I left the farm to attend a boarding school at Toowoomba Grammar. It was the first time I had been away from Mum and Dad and the farm. So for the first time in my life, I knew what it meant to 'go it alone' in many ways. This move was tough financially for my parents, but boarding school was the only option. The nearest local secondary school was in Tara, an hour's drive each way with no school bus service.

The fact that my parents really had to struggle to send me to school created an expectation on me that affected my future for a long, long time. There were always innuendos about having to perform and do well. I remember on my very first maths exam, I got 14 out of 20, which in Dad's eyes was a failure. At the time I thought, 'How on earth am I going to explain this to Dad?' I worked my arse off after that. I thought, 'I just can't let him down and I just have to work harder.'

Some may consider this a harsh upbringing. My view is that it established early on a pattern for me of doing all things very well. While I had to work through my fears of failure and disappointing my father, this mindset aided me in the long run. Life is what you make of it, and your perspective on your situation will either positively or negatively affect your life and work. It is all about choices. Choices of our own making.

So I became pretty much a straight-7 student after that. The system then was Gradings 1-7, with 7 being the best grade achievable. I did well but not just in Year 8 (my first year of secondary school). All the way through secondary school I got 7s for almost everything. English, I think, let me down with a 5. The irony was mathematics ended up being my best subject. And I ended up taking Advanced Maths all the way through.

I think the good marks at school were a combination of the natural work ethic that had been etched through those hard days on the farm, my father's pressure and something inbuilt that made me work hard. There was no doubt Dad ruled through fear. So for me it was always a case of 'I can't let him down; I will suffer the consequences if I do.' And he certainly wielded the cane. Growing up in that environment, and seeing Dad work hard as he did – and me out there doing it with him– also created a strong work ethic. I still carry that ethic today.

I was twelve years old when I started at Toowoomba Grammar, and I felt like the kid amongst all these senior guys. It was a very old school with a total of only 300 boarding students, many of whom had grown up together so they had known each other for many years. My perception of being smaller stemmed from the 'new kid on the block' syndrome. Time eventually resolved most issues that arose and left behind lessons that built up my emotional strength as my inner support system was all I had to draw on.

That first year I experienced a lot of homesickness. There was of course your typical boarding school initiations and bullying. The school didn't condone it, but it happened. I don't think I fared any worse than others. I started boarding school as one of the smaller children, but I grew quickly, so by Year 9 I was one of the bigger kids and maybe that helped keep the bullies away.

A highlight of boarding school was sport. I loved sport and had been involved from an early age, even at Hannaford where I would compete in primary athletics meets. I used to do a bit of running, cross country and swimming. In primary school I thought I was a handy sprinter. But by the time I was at boarding school, I realised it was something quite different. I wasn't a sprinter at all, more of a middle-distance runner. I was always interested in sport and to this day I still watch sport.

At boarding school there seemed to be almost every sport on offer – cricket, rugby, athletics. Ironically that was a 'negative' in my grandparents' eyes. They saw Toowoomba Grammar as a 'sports school' that did not place enough emphasis on academics. But I loved it and played every sport I could. In summer it was primarily cricket and then in the winter months it was always rugby. I continued as a middle-distance runner – 800m and 1500m – in the athletics season with some solid results. Since Toowoomba Grammar was a Greater Public School (GPS), the competition was high.

Those who attended GPS schools were considered to be part of an elite group of students in Queensland as not everyone could afford to attend such a school. So there was a definite level of prestige that flowed through to the students. Often students who attended our school were offered sports scholarships and this program assisted the school in establishing their sporting profile. This in turn usually contributed to a higher achievement level.

Rugby was the sport I excelled at. I was always an A-Grade player in rugby union in all my age groups, right from the get-go. I played in the forwards, firstly as hooker, and then as I grew I moved into the second row. By the time I had reached my mid-teens, I was bigger than most kids my age. A lot of my friends were leaner, smaller, but I just kept growing and filling out. I was always on the verge of being selected for rep teams but always 'just' missed out.

Deciding Next Steps

I attended Toowoomba Grammar for three years until the end of Year 10 and then, at fifteen years of age, it was my decision to leave and attend Longreach Pastoral College. I know that decision was a big disappoint-ment for Mum and Dad, particularly Dad, because he wanted me to go right through to senior at Grammar and then on to a university. But I was adamant that my future was in going home to the farm. I told them that since my plan was to work on the farm, then attending a regular school, such as Toowoomba Grammar, would not be of any value whatsoever. I would rather go to an 'Ag' college and learn to be a farmer.

I protested quite strongly. My mind was made up. The teachers at Grammar were counselling me, saying, 'You are an above average student. You are getting 7s and 6s. You should stay on and go on with this.'

This was one of the first times I really stood my ground with Dad. I remember it being scary because my parents were adamant I should stay at Grammar. And being in open disagreement with Dad had not been part of my life thus far. But I fought really hard for what I wanted . . . and obviously won. I know it was a disappointment for them, but then I didn't let them down at Longreach because I ended up being at the top of my class there as well.

And so I passed a vital test I'd set for myself. I'd stood up to my father and did what I needed to do to achieve the future I wanted. In this moment, I learned to have courage and confidence in myself. I recall facing a lot of opposition for my decisions. Although staying at Grammar might provide some value for him on the farm with my additional academic learning, the farming training would contribute so much more in other ways. When I explained this to him, I also refused to continue more academic learning.

My father was also struggling with his desire for me to be the first grandchild in the family to attend a university. He and his family believed that the next generation should do better than the last. How would it look to the family if I pulled out of academic studies and went back to the farm? On the other hand, he also wanted me to come back to the farm to help out and have it pass through the generations. Perhaps I realised this subconsciously as I used that argument to convince him to let me do what I wanted.

Eventually he conceded, realising that my success at Longreach would most probably bring me back to the farm after marrying, as was the norm in those days. He accepted compromise as a positive move in the end and consequently was less controlling in my final decision. This enabled me do what I needed to do.

Longreach Pastoral College was well known and respected as a good stepping stone for young people who intended to live off the land. I had a ball there. I really loved it. A lot of the curriculum was actually practical work out on cattle and sheep stations. We were breaking horses in. We were doing anything that a ringer or jackeroo did. I learned to shear a sheep there. In fact I used to shear stragglers for pocket money on weekends at nearby sheep stations. And then, of course, we had the theory and were taught about actual farming. Those two years were very beneficial and I graduated in 1976 at the age of seventeen.

This experience of standing behind my own beliefs and even risking of the wrath of my father to fight for them proved to me that taking a stand was the right thing to do.

So it was time to move on to adulthood – to recognise that my decisions had consequences, that I had the power to create change and that I needed to take responsibility for the changes I made.

Something to Ponder

Are there actions you do today, even subconsciously, that point to the fact that your past continues to affect your future (either positively or negatively)?

What do YOU believe in?

Do your actions support those beliefs or do they only fall in line with mainstream or socially acceptable behaviour?

ONCE AN ADULT, ALWAYS AN ADULT

Once an Adult,
Always an Adult

'Seek not outside yourself, for all pain comes from a futile search for what you want, insisting where it must be found.' A Course in Miracles

'You don't have any problems. You only THINK that you do.'
A Course in Miracles

A Podiatrist Becomes an Adult

Realising I needed to take responsibility for dropping the ball on my TE scores, I decided to fund my studies at night school. So I started working at a news agency at the Garden City Shopping Centre. I worked there full-time, and at nights I studied accounting and ancient history at night school. I chose those subjects as low-hanging fruit that would have the largest impact on my grades.

After twelve months, I was able to push my TE score up to 980, allowing me to pursue a Bachelor of Applied Science (Human Movements) degree at the University of Queensland. I had just missed out on doing physiotherapy but I thought I could upgrade to physio once I was in the system. Again, these were all steps in a learning process. If you want something and are prepared to work towards a goal and take the required action, then most times you will achieve your goal.

But although I was now in uni, I still did not have a clear idea of what I wanted to be. I thought I liked health and sport. So I considered physiotherapy or something in the area of sports health. But I decided to just start my degree, knowing that once you get to uni, you can upgrade and cross over to something else. I was happy I got in at all and human movements sounded interesting even though I had no idea what it could really lead to. It was an open-ended degree which had no direct alignment to any specific profession.

So I got into human movements and enjoyed myself. I definitely played up more than I should have, though, and didn't take things as seriously as I should have. I did enough to pass and just get through. Because of that, the four-year degree probably took me four and a half years of actual study to complete. All through high school I had worked weekends at the news agency and so I rarely went to a party or spent time with friends. So when I started at uni, my social life began in a lot of ways. I enjoyed myself more, trying to make up for lost time.

As I progressed through my degree, I started to ask those ahead of me what career options this could lead to. I found out that it went into two streams – exercise physiology and education. So for a long time I entertained the idea of doing one of those. And the more I talked to people, it just so happened that my close friends went down the education path. They said that if I went this way, I could still do all the exercise physiology that I wanted but still have the backup of teaching if I wanted to do it. That sounded like a good plan.

So I went down the education pathway but quickly realised I didn't enjoy teaching at all. Yet I wanted to finish what I started and get my degree while considering my other study options at the same time.

Still pondering my options, I decided to take a break and go overseas with a mate. This would give me time to think and decide what I wanted to do with my life. I applied for dentistry, optometry, podiatry, physio and audiology. The plan was to decide my career path while I was away and then continue studying along one of those strains when I came back. As it turned out, I was accepted into all of these programs except for audiology (because I didn't have a certain psychology prerequisite). I found myself approaching a crossroads in life, but I still wasn't ready to choose one path.

Observing Adversity

Just before I went overseas I was fortunate enough to get a job working at a maximum-security prison as a sports and recreation officer. A mate of mine from uni was working there and he told me how good the pay was ($30 an hour) and that all you did was play sport with the inmates. I was sold on the idea, applied and got the job. That was probably one of the most enlightening and challenging experiences I have ever had in my life.

The people I interacted with were 'on the inside' for murder, rape, grievous bodily harm, drugs, theft – anything and everything. Many of them were just teenagers from all walks of life. It made me realise how very, very lucky I'd been and how appreciative I was for the opportunities I had previously taken for granted. I got to know the inmates over time and I became friendly with a lot of kids who had done some pretty bad stuff. These were kids who I'd never have chosen to have any interaction with whatsoever on the 'outside'. But by working with them, I learned some incredible lessons.

I remember talking to a young bloke who had been institutionalised in some kind of facility since he was nine. He had a heroin addiction and alcohol dependency problems by the time he was ten. His sister had gone down a similar path. He had been in and out of jail for assault and different types of theft.

I asked him, 'Mate, how does this happen?'

He said, 'My earliest memory was Mum giving us nip of rum to shut us up and then the next thing we knew, we had drug addictions while we were in single figures.'

They never even had a chance.

My deep appreciation for my kind and good parents bloomed. Before that day, I used to focus on how difficult my childhood was, considering how we all had to work so hard and miss out on quality time as a family.

But now I saw my parents as they blessing they truly were. I did not realise how incredibly lucky Chris and I had been.

My new friends would tell me that 'when I get out next time, I am going to make a clean break and I am going to turn things around.' Two months later they would be back saying, 'I tried to do all the right things but, look, I don't know anyone, and it is so foreign, like a different country. So you go back to your support network and next thing you know, you go down the same road.' That's when I started to understand how integral your community is to your long-term success.

I worked there for a couple of years, and as my mate had said, the job amounted to organising and playing sport with the inmates. Keeping them busy. We used to play basketball, cricket and touch football. There were some amazing athletes in there. Every now and again you would worry a little bit about your safety, but generally for every six inmates there was one guard.

During some of the sports activities there were plenty of times you ended up face-to-face with someone special. One guy was particularly terrifying; psychologically he was not sound. He was in there for an horrific crime in North Queensland.

I remember playing basketball against him and he came charging through the key. I went up to block him and my elbow clocked him in the nose. Blood flew everywhere. I freaked out wondering what his reaction would be – and also what was in his blood? But he wasn't too upset about it. The guards rushed in and calmed him down and we went through the process of cleaning everything off. Some of the other inmates laughed it off and he ended up shaking it off.

As an observer there, I realised it was often the circumstances of their upbringing that brought the inmates to making poor choices. They were still people, just less fortunate than I had been. I recall how my Dad would condemn those who committed crimes; he would always dismiss any conversations I started after work about my day because they were 'criminals'. Another lesson learned while observing others.

That job was emotionally taxing because I was conflicted all the time. It was difficult to empathise with these guys who became career criminals – often because they felt safer on the inside. In their opinion, there was nothing for them in the outside world. I would have liked to have done more for them. But some people are not willing to change their ways.

On occasions that reality came like a slap to the face. I drove to prison each day in my own car. One day an inmate said to me: '317 NWC'.

I looked at him and said: 'What?'

He just said: 'That's your number plate, isn't it? I could find you when I get out . . .'

It was a different world. There was always the threat of danger.

Tasting Freedom

So in 1995 I was off overseas. I was twenty-two and had the world at my feet. The plan was to travel through the United States and Europe for a year. I went with a mate I was working with at the jail, Christian Hauff. For both of us it was the first time we had been overseas without family. We also had two mates joining us after they finished a stint in the UK. The idea was that we would buy a van and drive around the States. We had bought a one-way ticket from New York to London as well. I knew I had my studies and some sort of career to come back to. I had about $4000 to spend and was ready for the time of my life.

We were far from experienced, or even organised, travellers. The initial flight ticket was Brisbane – Sydney – Los Angeles. The day we were flying out, I thought: 'I had better pack my bag.' I started packing and soon realised my bag was far too small.

So I drove into the city to buy a bigger backpack and the salesperson said: 'So, when do you leave?'

I replied: 'In four hours.'

He just looked at me and said: 'Jesus, mate, you are cutting it fine.'

Anyway, I went back home, packed, and Mum and Dad drove me to the airport. Of course there was an accident on the way and so I had to fast-track the teary goodbye and run to customs. But when I got there – no Christian. He was even later than I was.

At the time he had a girlfriend who was practically living with him and, as he tells it, had her claws in so deep, she wouldn't let him to go. She was hysterical at the airport because there wasn't enough time to say a proper goodbye. But somehow we both made it onto the plane, only to realise that Christian had lost his passport. We found out later he had left it in the scanner at customs. There were some frantic negotiations and we were able to somehow get the passport to Sydney. But it was a very stressful few hours. And then we were on the plane to LA, and of course proceeded to do the responsible thing – get absolutely blind drunk. We were a bit excited.

So, we were drunk the whole flight. It is hard to imagine ever being happier than we were at this stage. We landed at LAX, went through customs and when we were on the 'other side', we sat down and I turned to Christian and said: 'So, where are we staying?'

His reply: 'I didn't book anywhere. Didn't you?'

So there we were, sitting on a bench out the front of LAX, still drunk, with no idea where we were going or where we were staying. Then, of course, the obvious happened! A bloke walked up to us right then and shouts: 'Hauffy!' It was a schoolmate of Christian's who just happened to work at a backpackers in LA and invited us to come and stay there. First problem solved!

We really were travel novices. When we walked into the backpackers, you could tell all the others had been 'on the road' for some time. Even their packs looked seasoned. And they had chains. Chains everywhere. The bags were even chained to the beds. So we went to sleep that night clutching our backpacks. No one was going to steal our bags during the night.

We stayed at the backpackers for a few days while we waited for our other two travel companions to arrive. We quickly realised that while overseas travel was a lot of fun, it was also expensive. We were running through our savings already. Some other backpackers suggested we go down to Mexico to a place called Puerto Vallarta, which apparently was a beautiful coastal city, and very cheap. So we bought a bus ticket and set off on the supposedly twenty-three-hour drive. That was one of the first things to go wrong on this trip. The bus trip took forty-eight hours to get there and still rates as the worst bus ride of my entire life.

And Puerto Vallarta, well, yes, it was beautiful, yet also . . . interesting. The four weeks that we were there deserve a book in itself. You quickly get used to Mexican police doing inspections with machine guns. Really quite confronting. And of course no one speaks a lick of English. But we were 'lucky' enough to meet a young bloke who, though a bit dodgy, took us under his wing and helped find us a place to rent. As promised by our friends at the backpackers, everything was cheap.

Our unit was close to the beach, Coronas were twenty-five cents and you could buy two litres of white spirits (vodka, gin or Bacardi) for eight bucks. What could go wrong? So we just drank all day at the beach and partied all night. We had an amazing time, awesome fun. As it turned out, too much fun. After about a week or so, we became really, really sick. Fortunately our apartment had two separate toilets. And that is where we stayed for a couple of days. We weren't getting much better so we asked around for a doctor. Language was always a problem.

Our Spanish consisted of *Hola*, *Pollo*, *Gracias*, *Tequila* and *Corona*, but we ventured outside our unit and got directions to a medical centre . . . which turned out to be right next door to us! The diagnosis? Montezuma's Revenge – which dates back centuries to when Spain was first invaded. Like us, the invaders enjoyed their new surroundings a little too much, and with it being so hot, they drank too much alcohol and didn't hydrate. So we were just severely dehydrated. Within a few days we were back in party mode.

Most nights we would go out to 'American' clubs. It was a great party atmosphere – lots of girls, lots of drinking and lots of fun. Compared to the locals, both Hauffy and I were tall, as most of the locals came up to about our shoulders. Now this was good for attracting the attention of girls, but bad for attracting the wrong kind of attention. So, one night we were out at a bar where there were a lot of local Mexicans. This night we paid a certain amount for all-you-can-drink. Which was really bad for me because I wanted to see how much I could drink. Then things went sideways. I ended up running around like a lunatic, making a nuisance of myself and subsequently annoyed a few people I probably shouldn't have.

Late in the night, I went into the toilets and when I went to walk out, I was confronted by a bunch of Mexican guys. I tried to push my way through. Next thing I knew, someone smashed a bottle into the back of my head, which dropped me. I remember thinking: 'I have got all my money on me' (which wasn't a lot, but it was all I had). I was drunk enough not to be terrified, but I was sober enough to realise I was in a really bad spot.

So I jumped to my feet and just hit what was in front of me and ran! I ran out the front door right into the security guard and of course he knocked me down as well. I got up again and continued running to a cab, jumped in and yelled at the driver, 'Go! Go! Go!' I couldn't speak Spanish, the cabbie couldn't speak English and the 'bad guys' were now chasing us in their car. Somehow I got back to my apartment and lost my new Mexican friends along the way. But my problems weren't over.

The cabbie wanted a ridiculous amount as the fare. When I refused to pay, he called 'the Poliza'. Next thing I know I am on the ground in handcuffs with police machine guns aimed at me. I was then marched up to my room and I found enough money to pay the Poliza, as well as the cab driver. Just as I paid all them, Hauffy arrived home. My face was a mess. I cleaned myself up, and in the morning Hauffy and I had a long chat. We concluded that we had probably pissed the wrong people off and it was time to bid farewell to Mexico.

I was still pretty sore and sorry and could not put up with another forty-eight-hour bus ride, so we flew Aeromexico back to the States. That was an experience as well – yep, chickens next to me on the flight. When I was on the plane, my head was really throbbing. We got to Los Angeles, and the headaches continued, so I decided to see a doctor. After X-rays they found that I had a fractured skull from where I had been hit by the bottle. The treatment was rest . . . and no flying.

By now our other two mates had arrived. They were two blokes from uni who were also keen to travel but had started their stint in the UK. We had decided on spending the next twelve months travelling around the United States. So we all chipped in and bought an old Dodge van which was to be our transportation and accommodations. The sleeping arrangements were tight to say the least. At 189cm, I was the shortest out of the four of us. There were two bench seats, the floor behind the front seats and then there was the luggage area at the back. The back was the best because you could sleep diagonally and almost stretch out. The rear bench seat was the next best and the floor was horrible. So each night the four of us would rotate.

Your only other option for finding comfortable sleeping accommodations was to 'pick up' a girl. That meant you didn't have to sleep in the van. So when it was your turn to attempt to sleep behind the driver's seat, the pressure was on to 'find a friend' for the night. And if one of the other boys did pick up, that meant you got bumped ahead in the order. It was an unusual sleeping arrangement, but it worked.

It really was an incredibly eventful year in the States. We went around the West Coast. The first port of call for the four of us was down to Santa Cruz and Santa Monica. And of course, my habit of needing medical assistance continued. Wherever we were, we drank a lot. One night in Santa Cruz, we had more than a few and decided to go down to the beach. There was a footpath adjacent to the beach and a waist-high metal fence between the path and the sand. I decided to run and jump over the fence and as I did, I realised it was really quite a drop to the beach. I grabbed hold of the rail and tried to pull myself back up, and as I did so, I hit my leg on the edge of the cement wall.

Thankfully I was suitably anaesthetised, such that the knock didn't interrupt a very fun night. The next day, however, my leg was rather sore and I realised I had actually gouged a fair chunk out of my leg. I didn't think much of it and hoped it would heal up, and off we went to Vegas where the good times continued.

Once in Vegas, we didn't have enough money to stay on 'the strip', and I soon realised that in the States there isn't a great deal of distance separating the 'really nice' areas and the 'not so nice' areas. So we ended up in a mediocre resort we called 'Badsville'. While there I noticed my leg was starting to get a little bit inflamed and the wound was not healing.

Nevertheless, true to form we played up there for about ten days and then headed off to the Grand Canyon, which was amazing.

After leaving the Grand Canyon and making our way up to Salt Lake City, I started to feel pretty crook. The wound on my leg was now weeping profusely and I was drifting in and out of consciousness. Upon arriving in Salt Lake City, I was admitted to a hospital with severe cellulitis that was tracking rapidly up my right leg. The infection had already progressed from my mid-shin to above my knee. Each day the medical staff would draw a line on my leg to monitor the tracking of the infection. I was told that if the infection reached my groin, there was the possibility that I could lose my leg. And every day the infection would climb a little higher.

On top of my concerns regarding potentially losing my leg, money was a massive issue. I did have basic travel insurance in place, but costs were rising. Just the intravenous drip bags were three hundred dollars each (I asked) and I was having three of those a day. After a week or so, I was able to get myself discharged and each day I took an intravenous drip bag back to our unit where I hooked it myself up. I was now scared that I was going to lose my leg and I remember saying to Hauffy: 'I have got to call my mum.' He told me to wait until I was okay, as there was no point worrying her until we knew for sure what was going to happen. As it turned out, it was great advice. The infection stopped just short of my groin. I was on crutches for a while and my leg withered. But I survived with my leg intact!

I soon started to feel better and our adventure continued. From Salt Lake, we travelled through to Idaho and so on. We lived out of the van and also spent a lot of time at universities and colleges using the gym facilities and showers. The other three guys loved basketball and AFL. They weren't sports that were necessarily my go, but we 'played ball' and 'kicked the footie' wherever we went.

Desperate Times, Desperate Measures

The next stop was Vancouver. There our van was broken into and we lost almost everything. When I say broken into . . . we got really drunk one night and one of the guys, Adam, fell asleep on top of the van. The rest of us headed out, leaving the van wide open. We came back and the van was empty, cleaned out. And Adam was still asleep on the roof. That's when we found out that travel insurance really is worth having. We got a fair bit of money back and I was informed that my entire hospital bill was covered.

By this stage, we were running low on cash and one of the boys came up with the 'brilliant' idea that we could make some money by being gigolos. We actually spent a fair bit of time exploring the concept. A couple of problems presented – our clothes were pretty crappy by this stage of the trip and we didn't shower as regularly as I would have liked. And of course, it would always have to be 'an away game' as it would be a bit hard to entertain in the van.

With that career path extinguished, we decided on trying our luck at the skiing Mecca – Whistler. We were able to secure employment, roofing for a company looking after all the A-frame chalets in the valley. Those were long, tough days but it was fantastic to be finally earning some money again.

We still slept in our van and it was starting to get very cold. So we decided to drive across to Toronto before we ran out of time. We stopped in Calgary and then we went down to Chicago. There we stayed with two girls whom the boys knew from the UK and slept on their lounge room floor. Each day in Chicago, we went to a nearby field and played basketball with some local fellas and kicked the footy. We taught the locals how to play force-'em-backs – a kicking game played with an AFL football back home in Australia.

One day, one of the girls we were staying with asked us where we went each day. We told them about the field and the basketball court. They almost went white with fear. They told us to never go back there because that was gang territory and there were drive-by shootings there all the time. But we kept going. The locals called us Larry Bird 1, 2, 3, and 4 (after the American basketball player). They were all African American and nice fellows. But one day there was a shooting at the basketball court . . . we didn't go back the next day.

At this time the premier American basketball team was the Chicago Bulls. One of their players was an Australian – Luc Longley. We managed to get tickets to a Bulls game. Our seats were in 'the nosebleeds', as the Americans describe seats way up in the back. But we didn't care. This was another great experience for us. We arrived at the stadium early and the Bulls were on court doing their pre-game practice. All the stars were on show – Pippen, Rodman, even Jordan and of course our man, Luc Longley. We started yelling out, 'Luc! Luc! Luc!' Believe it or not, Longley looked up saw the Aussie flag we were waving and called us down to the court. Serious! This actually happened!

I have recounted this story MANY times and every time I get goose-bumps. Luc called us down to the court, introduced himself and started chatting away about our trip. He then asked where we were sitting and we pointed to the back of the stadium. Longley then says: 'Leave it with me.' Then he had to go and get suited up for the game and we climbed back to our seats thinking, 'What a great guy to take time out to talk to us.'

But our brush with fame wasn't over. Far from it. Just before the game started, a stadium official came to us and said our seats had been 'upgraded'. We were walked down to the second row, directly behind the Bulls' bench! We could almost reach out and touch stars such as Michael Jordan. At one stage during the game, Luc was on the bench beside Dennis Rodman. The Aussie turned to us and asked, 'How are the seats, boys?' We gave him a big thumbs up. And Rodman turned and gave us a wave. I can't even remember who the Bulls played or what the result was.

After the game had finished, Longley asked us to wait around while he got changed. He then told us that 'the boys' were going to a local bar. He asked us to come along and to tell the security the 'password', which we did and were allowed in. Longley told us he had to head home, but we looked across and there was Rodman at the bar surrounded by a bunch of women. He looked up and saw us and beckoned us over. So there we were, just four Aussie guys, sitting at a bar, having a laugh with Dennis Rodman and his groupies. What a surreal night.

Deciding the Future – What If

From there we travelled back to Toronto . . . and decision time. The four of us were good mates, but we had been living in each other's pockets for about eight months. By this stage we were starting to get on each other's nerves. It was time for 'the band' to disband and head in different directions. My choice was to either continue on to England or to go back to Whistler. I had always wanted to experience the full ski season, so Whistler it was. I shook hands with the other three, and then there was a fair bit of hugging and backslapping, and I flew off to Whistler by myself.

My three mates and I had a great time travelling and we will share lifelong memories, but for one reason or another we haven't stayed in touch. Christian kept in contact for about a year after, but even we drifted apart. Perhaps it was a period of my life that became compartmentalised. And then I moved on to another stage.

That 'stage' started with a job as a lift operator at a Whistler resort. It was a real contrast to what I had been doing – spending the previous eight months living in a mobile shoebox with three mates. The other lads weren't as keen to work on the mountain. Cracks were starting to appear in the group and we were starting to drift into different directions, especially me. That didn't matter now, though, because the ski season was still a couple of months away.

I had never lived completely on my own before so I looked forward to the whole experience. Another lesson coming up for me – going it alone. My employers organised accommodations for me and I thought it would be great to meet a whole bunch of different people hopefully from different countries. I was put in a share house with ten people. It was an amazing house. As it happened, eight of my housemates were Australian. So it wasn't quite the multicultural experience I had hoped for.

Yet Whistler was a great experience. A lot of fun. Long, cold days and early starts, but I met some really, really good people. Ironically, even though we were in a big share house with crowds of people around, I still spent a lot of time by myself and learnt to enjoy my own company. I also rediscovered my love of reading and journaling – activities I normally didn't have the headspace to do.

I spent almost a full ski season there – about four months – and it was fantastic. Nearing the end of the ski season, I was tossing up whether to finish the season, fly to England and continue my travel odyssey, or return home and go back to uni. It was one of those sliding doors moments. At this stage, I was getting homesick and missed my brother, parents and friends badly. I'd decided I was ready to go home – and that I wanted to pursue podiatry.

I was at the crossroads, trying to figure out what I wanted to do with my life. Even to this day, I still wonder what would have happened if I had gone to the UK, if I hadn't cashed in that one-way ticket from New York to London that I had purchased before I left home. But I will never know. At the time, I did agonise long and hard about that decision, but eventually I was committed to coming home and pursuing a career in podiatry. Whether I took the easy way out, I don't know. The lesson this time? How to cope with 'what if's.

Upon reflection, going to the UK was probably a step too far outside my comfort zone. Returning home and finalising a degree with a narrow career focus was a safe option in a lot of ways. It was time to sink my teeth into something.

So in early 1997, I was back on a plane and heading home. The twelve months of travel had been a magical experience, something that will always remain etched in my memory. Life is all about timing and that was a time to be young, silly and adventurous. But between the drunken nights, injuries and sight-seeing, there had also been a fair bit of growing up. I was ready to become an adult. It had been a long time coming.

I was now twenty-four, and it was really great to be home, to see everyone and to start the next stage of my life.

How could I have known what I was about to be faced with? Life was really only just beginning for me.

A Coach Becomes an Adult

By 1977, now an adult at eighteen, I was where I always wanted to be – back on the family farm. All the way through boarding school and Longreach Pastoral College, that was always my dream, to come home to the farm. That was all I knew, all I could think of. Even now, there are no regrets in terms of what I did and what I gave up to become a farmer. But reality soon set in.

I was maturing and I started to realise that I had been viewing our farm, and farming in general, through rose-coloured glasses. My perception of farming was that it was a beautiful lifestyle and although it had been fun while growing up, I knew nothing of the personal experiences of drought, financial anxieties and their implications, along with other hardships most farmers endure at some point. I had been taught about these things but didn't know what it felt like to experience them firsthand.

When I came back to the farm from Longreach, we were experiencing a very difficult drought and Mum and Dad still struggled money-wise. They couldn't afford to pay me and I recall being resentful that I didn't even have enough petrol to drive to town.

So really it was inevitable that I would have to leave. The farm could not support me as well as my parents. However I wasn't game to talk to Dad about the fact that I wanted to leave. I knew things were difficult for them. Although they couldn't afford to pay me, having an extra hand and strong back about was helpful.

The upside of it all was that even though I knew I soon had to leave, Dad had become proud of what I'd achieved at Longreach. So I carried no guilt for standing up to him back when I'd decided to pursue agricultural studies. I had performed very well.

My escape came through football. I loved footy. Every Sunday through the winter of 1977, I would play in Tara's A-Grade rugby league. Dad absolutely hated me playing because football was on a Sunday and if I turned up sore or injured on Monday, I either couldn't work or was restricted in how much work I could do.

So there were a lot of arguments between Dad and me about footy. However, during that season I had a potential offer to play and work in New Zealand the following year (1978). It was my little lever to say to Dad: 'Hey, look. I have an opportunity. I am going over to New Zealand and I am going to work and earn a bit of money. Then I will come back home again.' And that is the way it panned out. Just before Christmas 1977, I left home for my first major adventure.

Tasting Freedom

I travelled with a chap who promised me a rugby union opportunity and also a prospective job. It wasn't a confirmed contract at this point, but I felt it was worth pursuing. There was another opportunity in my lap at the time. I could have gone to the Middle East to drive oil tanker trucks. It offered good pay but was quite dangerous. So, decision time. Weighing up the pros and cons, even though the New Zealand 'offer' wasn't totally on the table yet, I felt it was closer to home and not as dangerous as the Middle East was at the time. My travelling colleague also had a cousin in New Zealand and I had no one in the Middle East, so I felt I took the easier and safer option. Choices. Another lesson learned – freedom also means having to make choices.

We flew into Wellington. I had $100 in my pocket and no return ticket. Reality set in. We travelled to Wanganui where I was supposed to meet up with my employer and join the local rugby club. Unfortunately neither plan eventuated. As it turned out, the bloke I was travelling with had stretched the truth more than a little. This meant I was in a foreign country with a dwindling money supply. Now I had to get creative.

We were staying at my travelling companion's cousin's place in Wanganui. I know we were leaning pretty hard on her because I had no money and no job at the time. I remember her instigating some difficult conversations along the lines of, 'You two have to move on.' I did eventually get a job making hay – difficult manual labour.

I never did play rugby over in NZ. That was a pity because I had always had sporting aspirations. When I was playing football for Tara,

I was playing A-Grade and trying out for some rep teams. At that age, I believed I could make the grade at the elite level at either rugby code. I had friends who did just that – played first grade rugby league in Brisbane. Graham McCullough (whose son Andrew currently plays for the Brisbane Broncos), Selwyn Murphy and Russell Neil were three who did just that.

So the New Zealand adventure turned sour, including the hay-making job. The bloke who employed me went broke and I ended up not getting paid for my work. I was then able to get a job at a wool store. This was the first time in my life I was owed money and didn't get paid for it. And even worse, the little red flags had been flying high all along, but I'd ignored them. I trusted people too much without doing my due diligence and getting all the needed facts. Note for self – trust 'red flag' feelings in the future and find out more facts.

However there was one positive to the New Zealand experience. I met my first wife there. That meeting came at a time when I was getting desperate money-wise. I was at a party and someone introduced me to Sharon. There was a big age difference. I was eighteen and she was nine years older, but we hit it off straightaway. I ended up lobbing on her doorstep and she allowed me to stay there. She was flatting with a girlfriend whom she worked with at a car dealership in Wanganui. The flatmate moved out after a few months of my being there, though. She probably felt disenchanted with Sharon spending more time with me than her.

By mid-1978 I decided I had had enough of NZ and trekked back to the farm at Hannaford. Sharon came back with me. I hadn't told Mum and Dad that I was returning with 'a friend'. So all of a sudden I appeared with this woman. By this time they had moved from the shed after building the house, but to say things were 'uncomfortable' would be a major under-statement. The fact that I appeared with a woman they knew nothing about was bad enough, but the fact that she was nine years older than me? Well, that was controversial, to say the least.

To ease the congestion, before too long Sharon and I bought a caravan, plonked it on the farm and lived there for several months. But eventually the whole situation just became unsustainable. Dad and I were fighting. I was working on the property, but again he just couldn't afford to pay me or manage the costs of the farm. The financial pressure had become a real issue for Dad and the fact that he just couldn't accept Sharon placed additional emotional strain on everyone. What would other people think? He also felt threatened by his son moving into the first phase of his life. So there was a lot of anxiety.

I remember one occasion where Dad and I literally faced off against each other while we were out droving cattle between our two properties. I had done something with the cattle that he didn't agree with. So I reacted to his temper, and there we were, fists raised, ready to fight. We then both realised what we were doing, backed off and walked away. We never spoke about that again. It was just one of those moments for me when I realised, 'Okay, this is not going to work'.

Sharon and I had to leave the farm, which meant I needed a job. About that time the deputy principal from the Longreach Pastoral College had been appointed as principal for the brand-new Dalby Agricultural College. I knew him through my days at Longreach and I contacted him about the possibility of working at the new college. Dad was actually in agreement that I should move on. There were no hard feelings. He knew the farm couldn't support us both and that I needed to go and start my own life.

When I look back on that period of my life, it's clear to me that my life choices were motivated by a desire to prove something to my father. At the time, I felt very independent since I'd graduated from Longreach and certainly felt like a real adult. Unfortunately my dream quickly soured into resentment when I returned to the farm and my dad still treated me like a child. I had completed my studies and couldn't understand why he didn't listen to what I had learned. Marrying Sharon also seemed to prove that I was now an adult. That backfired with Dad as he didn't agree with my choice of wife. It took me years to recognise that I had gotten married for the wrong reason – to prove to myself and Dad that I was growing up. Later I would also realise that all my efforts were in vain. I would always be a child in Dad's eyes. Another new learning again – the parent-child syndrome.

As it turned out, I did get a job at the Dalby Agricultural College towards the end of 1978. They weren't open at the time as the first class of students would arrive the following year. Initially my 'job' was helping knock the property into shape – a lot of manual labour. When the college did open, I was appointed as one of the staff members to help do the 'prac' side of the learning – how to drive a tractor, saddle a horse, etc. Meanwhile, Sharon and I rented a house in Dalby.

I was at the college for three years until 1981 when, at twenty-two years old, I left. Initially I enjoyed the work, but I grew despondent. The principal picked up on this and took me aside. He was very honest and explained to me that without any sort of formal qualifications – which I had none – there really wasn't a long-term career at the college for me.

He suggested I look for work that could be turned into a career path. At that stage I probably still had some aspirations of returning home to the farm, although those thoughts were waning. Once you get a taste of 'the other side' and earn a regular income, well, farm life sits more in perspective.

The income at the time wasn't great, but it wasn't bad either. It gave me a bit of freedom. Also, I didn't feel as though I had my father looking over my shoulder all the time. Now, I was still connected to the farm. Dad still expected me to come home every weekend to work. That sparked a few arguments. But I found myself gradually breaking further and further away from home and creating my own life.

Deciding the Future – What If

That life included getting married. I was now twenty-two years old and had finished my education (at least I thought I had). I was about to find out that it is not only at school or college that our education is learned.

Sharon and I were married in 1981. She worked in secretarial administration at Engine Rebuilders in Dalby. At the time, financially we were doing okay. Two incomes. It was such a contrast from the constant financial pressure that surrounded life at my parents' place. However with my time at the Dalby Agricultural College coming to an end, I realised I had to get some sort of qualifications and find another job. So the choice was – do I go back to uni? Again, I had only completed Year 10 so technically I was short on qualifications for that. Or, do I continue to work and do an external course as a mature age student? I chose the latter.

The challenge then was to find a job that could support me through that stage. I applied for a few positions, eventually making it through to an interview. The sales manager for that firm who interviewed me started talking about a few things the position required. However one of my very first questions was – what was his view towards extra studies? The response was favourable and so that sold it to me straightaway. There was one problem. After six months in the field research position I was applying for, I would be out on the road selling. But I had an ingrained dislike of travelling salesmen.

All through my life growing up on the farm, that idea had been force-fed to me. Dad even had a sign on the gate: 'No Hawkers Allowed'. So when the job interview went in that direction, it was like a little knife being driven into me. However that was negated by my overpowering urge to find a job that would allow me to study. I told myself, 'Okay, let's give it a go and maybe I can even fudge the selling part.'

So in late 1981, I started work for Consolidated Fertilisers (CFL). At that stage the company was wholly owned by ICI. That company evolved into another organisation called Incitec and is now Incitec Pivot. Initially my job entailed doing field research – running fertiliser trials on farmers' properties in the Darling Downs and Central Queensland. This was basic farm work. I would be on the road with a tractor on the back of a truck.

Our local rep would organise with farmers for me to come along, plough mark out a plot on each farmer's property and plant a trial crop using our fertiliser. We would maintain the plots during the growing season and then come back and harvest them and measure the end result. Most of the time the farmer could see how successful our product was. The 'work' was what I had grown up doing. I had been on a tractor ever since I was a child.

As soon as I started with Consolidated Fertilisers, I also started studying. I applied for enrolment at the Darling Downs Institute of Advanced Education and also Armidale University and was accepted into both. With Armidale, I was accepted into an economics degree and at Darling Downs it was a commerce degree.

I decided to study through the university, purely because I believed a university degree would hold more credibility. The course was a Bachelor of Economics, not that I wanted to do economics, but again, it was simply a ticket. I knew once I was enrolled and accepted that I could change the degree, which is exactly what I did. I converted that degree into account-ing after the first year.

Looking back, I certainly worked hard on my studies. I spent quite a bit of time on the books each week. I set a load of two units a semester for myself and would get up at 4am and study. I tried to avoid night study, but occasionally I would have to burn the midnight oil. Weekends I used to put towards assignments – and there was a lot of assignment work. In all it took me seven years to complete the degree including a year off. It was tough and at one stage I nearly gave up.

The balance between all the study and a long day at work was hard. I would often be tired by the end of the day. After experimenting with my schedule, I found that getting an early start was imperative. I would get to work right away and be productive. But towards the end of the day, it got a bit hard. That habit of waking up early to get to work has developed into a routine that's become enormously successful for me. I was learning what it means to be a confident, independent and self-reliant man – a valuable lesson since in the months to come, I wouldn't be the only person relying on me to get the job done right. The burden of responsibility was about to get a lot heavier.

Something to Ponder

Do you have faith in yourself to trust your own judgement?

Don't be frightened to step outside your comfort zone. Back yourself and your own decisions. If it feels like it's the right thing to do for you, do it.

THE IMPACT OF
RELATIONSHIPS

The Impact of Relationships

'Some of the biggest challenges in relationships come from the fact that most people enter a relationship in order to get something: they're trying to find someone who's going to make them feel good. In reality, the only way a relationship will last is if you see your relationship as a place that you go to give, and not a place that you go to take.' Anthony Robbins

'The best and most beautiful things in the world cannot be seen nor even touched, but just felt in the heart.' Helen Keller

A Podiatrist Learns About Relationships

After returning from my overseas escapades, the decision to continue on at university at Queensland University of Technology (QUT) and embrace podiatry was not taken lightly. I had options. Physio? I thought, there are just so many physiotherapists out there. Dentistry? That would mean another five years of education. Optometry? Didn't really float my boat. So podiatry was the choice. And I had some friends who were currently studying podiatry and they spoke highly of it as a career and the opportunities available.

Podiatry was a four-year degree, but because I had a Bachelor of Applied Science in my pocket, I was entitled to quite a bit of credit – the equivalent of a year and a half. I had hoped that with the credit I would be able to condense the degree into three or even two and a half years. However QUT wouldn't allow me do that because this was actually the first year of the four-year degree. So it had to be done over four years, but because of my credits, certain semesters were a really light load.

Even though I had already spent four years at university, the prospect of another four years there didn't really worry me. I was determined to get this degree done and begin my career as a podiatrist. At the time, I regretted finishing my first degree (Human Movements) and not upgrading to a more specific course. But I made that decision with the information I had at the time and here I was, ready to go again. This time would be different.

University the second time around suited me more – or maybe I suited uni more. I have no doubt I had matured as a result of my overseas travels. Well, you would hope so, because the bar was pretty low to start with. Although I was older than a lot of the people in my year, I really enjoyed it. Previously I did just enough to get by, but now I was particularly motivated to do well. Podiatry resonated with me. This career was something I wanted to do. As a result, I went to lectures, I listened, I studied and I did well – I did really well. I had a totally different mindset. During my previous degree, it was about trying to figure out what I wanted to do, whereas this is pursuing what I wanted to do.

Because of my earlier achievements with my human movements degree, I was already a qualified teacher. I could actually go into a classroom and teach. Scary. What were they thinking? Although I was 'qualified', there is no way I thought I should be teaching. But it seemed a good way to earn money during my second degree. So I started substitute teaching at a couple of high schools – just filling in where needed in everything from English, maths, science and PE. It was good fun and not too difficult.

The experience did confirm, though, that I was not a teacher and I never wanted to be one. So I steered away from teaching and went back into the bottle shops and pubs to pay my way through university.

Now the podiatry degree was not a walk in the park and it was certainly more intense than human movements. Despite what was involved, I actually found it easier because I was genuinely interested and invested in podiatry. While studying Human Movements, I think my focus was primarily just getting by and having a great time. I was successful at both. Whereas with podiatry, I had a more specific and worthwhile focus. I had clarity that this was what I wanted to do.

As a result, it was much easier to concentrate because I knew I was working towards something specific. It was still a lot of work because there were a lot of medical subjects and a lot of high-end science material which could be a bit testing at times, but my renewed focus carried me through. Subsequently, I went from a GPA of 4.5 (out of 7) in human movements to 6.2 in podiatry.

The Benefits of Adversity and Maturity

What really appealed to me about podiatry was the fact that I already had experience in the field, having had a lot of lower limb injuries and pain growing up. Podiatrists helped me significantly during that time, so I knew firsthand the benefits the profession offered. As I progressed through the course, I was amazed at the impact I could potentially have on people's lives. I was in the right place.

With certainty around where I was going and the satisfaction of knowing I would make a difference, I enjoyed my time at QUT. Maturity was also a significant factor. When I was studying human movements, I was eighteen to twenty-two years old, but I probably had the maturity of a sixteen-year-old. So by the time I got to my second degree, I probably had the maturity of a twenty-year-old. I was still a few years behind.

Commitment – the Big C

Up until I started studying podiatry, I had never really had a serious relationship of any description. I was too busy having fun. In my second year of podiatry, this was to change. Then I met Lisa. Lisa was also in her second year of podiatry and we got to know each other pretty well over time. Long story short, we started seeing each other. Up until this point, I had never ever stuck with anything, particularly intimate relationships.

After a few weeks, I was getting the same old urge to break things off and return to what I knew and was most comfortable with, being by myself. The problem was I was actually starting to really like Lisa; she was smart, beautiful, determined and funny. I remember thinking to myself, 'Grow up, Troy! You are twenty-three. You like this girl. Give it a fair crack!' So I did. And it was great. There was only one problem: we would fight. We would fight . . . a lot. I kept blaming myself for the fights. I would second-guess myself and wonder if the fights were caused by my subconscious trying to rescue the situation and restore the equilibrium, that is, get back to single life. So I pushed on. We still fought. In retrospect, we just weren't suited.

I remember a mate of mine saying: 'Parso! You have got to put a bullet in this relationship. No one fights this much.' So one day Lisa called me saying she really needed to talk to me and asked if she could come over to my place. I had no doubt she was about to dump me. I recall waiting for her and planning how that afternoon I would go down to my local pub, The Royal Exchange (RE), catch up with my mates and get back to the single life. So, Lisa arrived, sat down, and said: 'I have something to tell you . . . I am pregnant.'

To say this announcement was a massive shock would still be a significant understatement. We had been going out for just five months and as it turned out, Lisa was about four months pregnant. This was March 1998. I was twenty-four and Lisa was twenty-two, both of us in the second year of a four-year degree. Now, Lisa had the maturity of at least a thirty-year-old; me, on the other hand, I was wallowing somewhere in my teens. I was a man-child. Initially I could feel myself drowning in this situation. No way was I ready to be a capable father. I was flat out looking after myself. I was in my second year of a university degree and I was only earning a couple of hundred bucks a week, working in a pub. How the hell was I going to raise a child and still complete my degree?

Over the following days, the panic subsided and Lisa and I began looking rationally at our options. I remember going around to Mum and Dad to tell them. Dad isn't a great communicator, but he knew immediately that something was troubling me. When I told them, Mum was the one who was shocked, whereas Dad just looked at me reassuringly and said: 'What can we do to help? What do you want to do? What do you need?'

So Lisa and I explored our options. We talked to a lot of people. Friends, associates – older people who had been through different life experiences. Ultimately we both decided we wanted this baby and the only practical solution was to move in together and make a real go of being parents and raise our new beautiful baby girl – Ana – together. At that stage we didn't talk marriage. And, in retrospect, if I was honest, I knew that I would struggle to live the rest of my life with Lisa. We just weren't compatible. But for Ana, we tried to make a go of it.

Lisa was living in a unit her Dad owned while he worked overseas, so I moved in there with her. It was a beautiful two-bedroom unit that overlooked the Brisbane river. Lisa's younger brother, Mark, also lived there. So although the unit was spacious, the reality was it was tight. Mark was in one bedroom and Lisa, myself and baby Ana on a cot shared a room. We would put Ana to sleep on the cot in our room and then when we went to bed, we would move her out to a port-a-cot in the lounge room. That is how we lived for the next couple of years as we finished our respective podiatry degrees.

Taking Responsibility for Our Actions

Ana was born on October 13, 1998. This was two weeks before the start of our final exams for the year. One of our lecturers suggested to Lisa that she should probably not do her end-of-year exams, having just had a baby, and that she continue with her studies the following year. But Lisa said: 'No, I will still do my exams.' There was no way she could allow herself to fall behind the group. Lisa and I had our differences, yet it was a real testament to her character that she not only completed those exams, but she did really well. When Lisa sets her mind to something, there is nothing she can't do – especially if you suggest she can't do it. 'Respect!' she'd reply. That said, the next couple of years were tough.

The logistics of two people trying to finish a degree, being new parents and also working part-time were something in itself. As a result, we had to enrol Ana into day care from day one. We would drop her at the university day care at 7am. We would then go straight to the library to study, as it was the only opportunity that we were likely to have. We would go to lectures, study again, pick up Ana and go home. There wouldn't be time to study at night. I would then go to work at the pub doing four or five shifts a week. And that was our 'program' for a couple of years – through 1999 and until we graduated at the end of 2000.

We probably both deserve credit for sticking at it through that period, both as parents and students. Our relationship was rocky to say the least. We fought a lot, more than we did pre-Ana, but that wasn't a surprise. We would have a fight and then Lisa would kick me out. I would always end up at Mum and Dad's place or at either of my mates' places, Derek or Fraser. I would just show up at their door at some point needing a bed.

Then there were times when the day care was closed and we would have to attend uni with Ana in a baby capsule. So our peers, friends and lecturers actually got to know Ana quite well over time. When I think back, I don't know how we did it. Despite us not being overly happy with each other, it was a testament to both Lisa and I that we were able to get through that period of our lives, still together, with our baby and with two degrees. In a lot of ways, it set us up for the rest of our lives, because it was a massive test.

We were just doing the best we could to get through uni and raise Ana. Now I love Ana more than I can describe, but she wasn't the easiest of babies. The nights were the hardest. Somehow she could sense when we had an exam, because the night before, Ana would refuse to sleep. We would try everything. I remember placing her in her capsule and I would lean my head against the wall, swinging the capsule back and forth, saying, 'Please sleep, please sleep, please, God, go to sleep'. And she wouldn't. It was just awful. I remember one night putting the capsule on the washing machine because the washing machine was going and she went to sleep. The next night I tried the same thing – didn't work. Nothing worked twice.

Life continued like this until we both finished university, when choices were put in front of us both for our futures. I had been offered a great job in Toowoomba with the option to buy the practice in a couple of years. Lisa wanted to locum for the first couple of years after uni. She did not want to go to Toowoomba.

So I made the hardest decision of my life. I left and moved to Toowoomba. In my opinion we were only together because of Ana. We tried but we both knew deep down we did not belong together. I reasoned that the best thing for Ana would be for both of her parents to be happy, and this would not be the case if we stuck together. When Lisa refused to come to Toowoomba, I decided that it was time for me to go and end that chapter.

I will always be thankful that my first serious relationship produced our beautiful daughter, Ana. Lisa and I get on well now, but for a while the split was acrimonious.

Moving Forward While Looking Back

My wife Maree and I had known each other for a long time, more than ten years, before we were married in 2012. Until Maree and I started going out, my personal life had always been less than settled.

I met Maree in 2002 in Toowoomba. She was good friends with my girlfriend at the time. Maree was engaged and soon to be married. After the split with Lisa, I wallowed for a while and then decided I needed to move on. So I reverted to what I knew, being single, this time as a dad. I started going out with a friend of Maree's and this resulted in a long-term relationship of about five years. We even got engaged. Although this relationship ended, the big positive was that through it I became friends with Maree. I also became very good friends with Maree's husband.

During the time since we had first met all those years ago, I had split up with my fiancée, while Maree had married, given birth to two girls and then her marriage ended. Because we knew the same people, Maree and I would bump into each other every now and again, and I was still good friends with her husband. Initially we were just friends of friends, not close. But over time, and as both of our situations changed, we went from nodding acquaintances, to brief chats to real discussions.

The reality was we must have always had feelings for each other, but we weren't aware of them. For a long time, we had been in the same circle but always someone else's partner. Instead of ad hoc meetings, we progressed to catching up more and more, and the relationship grew from there. There was obvious awkwardness around our friendship. We had been in a relationship with other people who were, or had been, good friends of ours, so at a certain stage Maree and I had to decide whether what we had between us was something real and worth pursuing. We knew we would hurt some of those around us, but I was almost blinded to this reality. I was deeply in love with Maree. I had not felt like this about anyone in my entire life.

Eventually, we decided together that 'Yes, we do actually love each other; we'll stay together no matter what.' We, of course, each had children from previous relationships – Maree has two beautiful daughters (Ellie and Jessica) and I have Ana – so we both knew and understood the whole step-parent role. In 2013, our son Mack was born. In all relationships, there is inevitably some teething and that was also the case with Maree and I, but for me there are certainly no regrets. I am now with the woman I love, a fantastic mother, my best friend and we have four awesome children together. Rock stars, all four of them.

When Maree and I first met, she was a journalist at the Chronicle in Toowoomba. Over the years since, she has worked briefly in administration at my podiatry practice, in the Communications Department for Queensland Health and in recent years she was the Marketing and Communications Manager at St Vincent's Private Hospital in Toowoomba.

Once Mack was born, Maree continued to work for St Vincent's but in a part-time role. She also does some marketing work for my businesses and just recently has teamed up with two of her friends and their own business, The Event Group. They organise events for businesses and charities. The Event Group is in its infancy, but I am backing the girls to create something very special.

Maree is just an amazing person. She is very much a product of her upbringing. Her parents, John and Joan, are wonderful people – successful, driven and fantastic role models. You never hear them whinge or complain. They just get on and do it. More selfless and respectful people I have not met. And Maree is very much of the same ilk. She is also an incredible mother and wife. Maree was born to be a mum and somehow still has the time and capacity to love and support me.

She is a great sportsperson; in fact she excels at almost anything she puts her mind to. When she was young, she chose to focus on ballet and achieved a very high level in that before she suffered knee problems and had to give dance away. Up until then she was considering ballet as a career. It was then that she turned her focus to triathlons and again she excelled, representing Australia in her age group. Maree still enjoys triathlons. In fact that is the one thing she does for herself. Training is her time.

So much of Maree's time is taken up looking after others – the children, me, work and a long line of charities and community events. Despite this, somehow at 5am most mornings she heads off to the pool to train, often with Jess. I often make fun of her, calling her 'Rio' (after the Olympics) or refer to her and Jess as 'the Campbell sisters', Kate and Bronte (the famous Aussie swimmers). The funny thing is, if she still took triathlon seriously, I would be very interested to see how far she could go with it. But she does enough to keep herself happy and to beat most competitors.

Commitment = Two-Way Support

If I had to categorise Maree, one of the words I would use to describe her would be 'a people pleaser'. Now I don't mean this in a disrespectful way.

What I mean is that Maree will do whatever she can to please people and make them happy. Maree will say 'yes' too often and subsequently commit herself too much. In that regard, sometimes she doesn't have realistic expectations. She tries to do too much and where we see sixty minutes in an hour, 'Ree thinks there is about ninety minutes and tries to work accordingly.

Maree and I started going out when I was still having problems with the business, just before Greg came on board. So through that whole period of transition with the business and myself, Maree was pivotal to it all. She wasn't at the forefront, yet she was so important. She was the sounding board for all my issues. She was also the person who helped me believe in what I was doing. Maree backs me 100% in all my decisions. Her support is unwavering.

She very rarely doubts me, very rarely criticises. She believes and backs everything that I choose to do with regard to the family and business. I didn't realise this at the time, but having that support so close was huge. I had never had this before. This support was especially essential as within a short period of time, I went from having just Ana as being my responsibility to having three others, and then Mack making it five.

So with that many people in my care, I realised I had to start getting serious about making good choices and changing everything for the better. The pressure to deliver was intensified once I took on the responsibility of looking after Jessie and Elle. No doubt it was a testing time. Especially when I first moved in with 'Ree and the girls. I rented out my house and moved into an instant new family.

This was the most difficult period of our relationship – that whole dynamic of a 'new' person coming into the home. I am just so glad that we made it through and now I have this beautiful family. 'Ree has to take a lot of the credit here for steadying the ship and helping me achieve what I needed to achieve in business.

Hindsight – One of Life's Teachers

My own experience with Maree's daughters, Ellie and Jessica, highlighted to me what a great dad Bob had been to Chris and me. I didn't appreciate that at all growing up. And even now I can lose sight of it. It is a tough gig looking after someone else's children. You take on that responsibility, but sometimes, especially initially, you feel like the spare wheel. I feel like that less and less now, but nothing ever replaces a blood bond. Like all step-fathers, Dad would have faced his challenges, and Chris and I would have made it difficult for him, just being kids. But he has been a champion father.

Mum and Dad (Cheryl and Bob) owned news agencies through the most of our school life. They eventually sold the second news agency – Lytton Road – because they were well and truly burning out. They are quite different from me in that they are conservative and risk-adverse. Well, yes and no. I say they were risk adverse yet over the years they have started, bought and sold many businesses, never giving up and working incredibly hard. Not many people take on that level of risk.

What I really meant was that they saw hiring and trusting staff as too risky. As a result they could never really grow or take a break and they certainly never took holidays. They just worked hard. As hard as I have ever seen anyone work. This ethic was not lost on Chris or me. How Mum and Dad did what they did for as long as they did, I don't know. Dad was up at 2am for about fourteen years, seven days a week, with just two days off a year. That was a nightmare.

When they sold the news agency, they bought a cleaning contracting business. Unfortunately the original owners of the cleaning business were not completely honest in this transaction. Mum and Dad were supposed to buy a business that already had cleaning staff. However when they took over, no staff. I remember being overseas and calling Mum to say 'Hi', and she was in tears because the sellers had completely misrepresented what the business was about. But true to Mum and Dad's character, they took something that wasn't worth a lot, worked hard and built it up into something that was saleable and eventually sold it.

Next, they bought a small goods distribution business. Dad had a refrigerated truck and sold small goods from the eastern side of Brisbane, over to North Stradbroke Island. Again he worked hard and I am pretty sure they sold this for a small financial gain.

Their next business adventure was in management rights. They bought the management rights for a three-storey walk-up unit complex in Surfers Paradise, on the Gold Coast – a building called Anchor Down. They lived onsite. There was a similar scenario to the cleaning business – at face value, it looked like a good business. However, face value was again a wee bit deceptive. They took over about two weeks before the infamous 'Schoolies' carnival, when about 30,000 school-leavers descend on the Gold Coast for a couple of weeks of partying. The assistance Mum and Dad were promised from the previous managers did not eventuate.

And other support systems also were found lacking. I recall heading to the Gold Coast for the weekend to have a look at my parents' new venture. By then the Schoolies had arrived and it was just a nightmare. I drove home on the Sunday wracked with guilt because, again, Mum was in tears. I felt so bad leaving them to the mercy of these hordes of schoolies running amuck. It felt like leaving a beloved puppy at the pound. But again, they just put their heads down and ploughed forward. Like the news agencies, management rights are hard work; this building was 24/7 hard work. But sure enough, after a couple of years they had turned what they were doing into a profitable business. So much so that they were able to sell for a very good profit.

With that experience behind them, they decided to again invest in management rights, this time in the Landmark apartment building in Mooloolaba on the Sunshine Coast in Queensland. This was a big building – nine floors and 133 apartments, a significant investment for them. Initially they were the onsite managers, which again meant a packed workload.

I stayed there a couple of times and could see how stressful it was for them. Same story. They struggled early on but weathered the storm and made good money out of it, to the extent that they were able to put in onsite managers and move back to the Gold Coast in semi-retirement, making a good passive income.

I remain close to all my family. My Nanna is 90 (at the time of writing this book) and I still catch up with her every now and again. Despite her age, she is an astute lady. Pa died in 2002 and over the years I have really missed him being around. I wish he had been with us longer so that I could have gotten to know him better and pick his brain a bit more. I had a huge amount of respect for him from an early age. In fact Chris and I were always competing for his attention.

There was something about Pa. He was magnetic. He had such a strong personality. From what I understand, though, he was an incredibly hard man. He was old-school, a disciplined worker. In his younger days, he worked across a variety of jobs and made quite a bit of money out of pubs in Sydney. My uncle, Mum's brother, went into the pubs and bottle shops with Pa, which Mum would have loved to have been able to do. But Pa said: 'No. You are going to be a receptionist.'

The pub industry was no place for a woman, according to Pa. I think she would have revelled in that industry, or even something in health. Eventually Pa sold out of the pubs and he and Nanna moved to the Gold Coast, and I remember them having horse stables on their block. In his later life, Pa had a series of strokes and was unwell for a long time. They moved into a unit at Main Beach, where Nana still resides.

As Pa's health was failing, Nana moved him into an aged care facility. We visited him there once or twice and then Nana said: 'Look, I don't want you to visit him anymore. I want you to remember him how he was. How he is now is not your Pa.' His health continued to deteriorate and eventually he passed away.

Chris and I are very close but were typical brothers growing up – a lot of laughs and just as many fights. I was a bit of a dick to him a lot of the time – the bullying older brother. But as we grew older, we grew closer and closer. He is certainly one of my best mates. We would love to catch up more than we do. He has been incredibly supportive and encouraging, always ready with a fresh perspective on situations.

And because we both have an interest in self-improvement, we find ourselves discussing it together. Just like it took me a while to get some real traction in life, so it did for Chris. He's making good headway now, which has been really pleasing to see. When I was struggling with my business, I probably talked to Chris more than anyone. I certainly let him know when I was finding things difficult. Still, when things were at their darkest, I kept those struggles locked up. I had yet to learn my greatest lesson: the power of being vulnerable.

Recognising Self-Growth

Thinking back many years later, the whole Lisa/uni/Ana experience was my steepest learning curve in life. It taught me resilience. It taught me what I am capable of. It also forced me to have clarity around what I wanted in life. You get to the stage where you have had enough arguments, enough tears, enough stress and just let all that stuff go. I used to carry around a lot of tension and anger for whatever reason. Much of that has dissipated because over time I have realised that I have been through it all and I don't need to do that anymore. So it takes a lot to rile me up now.

Throughout my journey, there have been many challenging times. I have to thank Chris for introducing me to personal development. It started with him taking me to a Tony Robbins event in about 2003. I began to realise that we are not victims and we always have a choice as to how we respond to a given situation. I started looking within rather than just looking outward, blaming and reacting to what is going on in the world around me – to take a bit more responsibility for my life. Getting on the path of personal development and actually looking to live in creation rather than reacting against it became one of the biggest shifts I made during that time.

A Coach Learns About Relationships

I accepted the new gig with CFL in Moree, even though I wasn't totally happy with living in another remote location. Still I liked the idea of having my own sales area. So once again, compromise was required, and this time I had someone else to consider apart from just me.

At this stage, married life was okay. We fell into marriage simply because it was the next logical thing to do. Sharon and I had been together for a few years. Sharon was getting older, and we both wanted children. For several months we tried to start a family. But just before we moved to Moree, we learned that we couldn't have children. That was a major blow to us both. We did a lot of research, but the answer was the same.

Soon after that we were off to Moree. Neither of us were thrilled about the move. Sharon wasn't happy because she had a fairly secure job and loved it. She was still working for Engine Rebuilders at Dalby doing secretarial work, office management and bookkeeping. She had continued working there when we moved from Dalby to Toowoomba. She would drive to Dalby every day and after a while she found other people actually doing the same thing, so they car-pooled.

Fortunately I quickly began to enjoy the sales gig at Moree. The training the company gave me was second to none. For me, I was still at a stage in life where I could be influenced by the right sort of training. And the training I received then helped me to develop into more of a 'people person'. I was put into situations right from the get-go where I was literally introducing CFL to that area.

The company had little presence in that northern NSW region. I was their first rep there which meant I spent a lot of time cold-calling. I had to get into the car and just go and meet people. I didn't even know their names. Cold selling was way outside my comfort zone. So it taught me a lot. It taught me resilience – knowing that whatever happened, it was going to be okay. Of course I also had to deal with the odd occupational hazard of the travelling salesman. Dogs were the biggest problem. I learnt quickly – after being bitten a few times – to wind the window down before getting out of the car.

The learning curve in sales was steep but enjoyable. I quickly learnt the importance of being conversational and creating a conversation. Within a short period of time, I was able to start a conversation with anybody. First off, I knew that the farmer knew that I was a sales rep. Arriving on his doorstep in a car meant I was either lost . . . or a sales rep. But I knew what the farmer was thinking because I had been on his side of the fence. I could just hear it – 'Here he is, another bloody rep.'

However what tipped the situation in my favour was not only had I been in the farmer's shoes, but I could say, 'You know, we are the new kids on the block, so why not give us a go?' Over time and with hard work, I developed relationships with a lot of the farmers.

But I didn't get any real traction early. In fact, I remember we were in the middle of a drought in that region. So I used all of that time to get to know people. I would regularly get back onto their properties to say 'Hi' – not to sell anything but merely to build a relationship.

I used to say to them, 'When things turn, I'd like to think you'll give me a go.' And it worked. We developed that Moree district into the largest selling district in the whole of CFL at the time. At that stage I was selling fertilisers and agricultural chemicals north to just south of Goondiwindi, and west as far as there was any cropping, which in real terms was Collarenebri (about 130kms away). South, I would go to just north of Narrabri. And east, Warialda. It was a very large district. It wasn't uncommon for me clock up 1000km a week.

Never Give Up

The fact that I was from the land held some currency for me. There was a relatedness there, an immediate connection you could make. I wasn't a university graduate who was wet behind the ears, unable to hold a conversation about farm stuff. My guiding principle – and one of the guiding philosophies that I use even now – was the importance of persistence. Never give up. You just never know how close you are to the goal. You have to be resilient and persistent and stop taking things personally.

Rejection is part of the game. In the early days when someone said 'No', I would take that to heart, thinking, 'Maybe I am failing, not doing well.' No one likes rejection, but the truth was that people weren't in a position to buy. I was able to rationalise that and say, 'Okay, that is the way it is. In the meantime, I can build up my skill set. Maybe I can learn from this experience.'

During that early period I remember we had a visit from CFL's general manager at a function which was held at our home depot, in the big shed where we stored all our fertiliser. I recall being concerned at the time because we weren't performing well and obviously the company had made a heavy investment in terms of having people on the ground down there. I wondered if he had come down to sack me. Then the GM came up to me and asked if we could have a private conversation. This guy's nickname was 'Mad Dog'. He was a redhead and was known to be aggressive and forthright.

We went to a quiet part of the shed. He put his arm around me and said: 'You are doing all the right things. You just need to keep doing it and it will all happen.' Obviously we had to log all of our activity and he would have seen how busy I had been and how many farmers I had been talking to. It wasn't long after that the rains did come, literally. And things turned. And people did remember me. Very, very quickly the momentum built. Within two years we had built my region into the most profitable district for the whole of the company.

My starting salary at CFL was $14,000, which I thought then was pretty good money. When I began selling, that increased to just above $20,000, with a company car. There were also other added lump-sum increments whenever we hit a goal or had an annual review. I can remember getting a 10% wage increase as I continued to increase my sales volume. Life was getting comfortable.

Sharon was still working then as well. She was working for a legal firm in Moree. With a double income, we were doing okay. We bought a house down there, but we never planned to stay in the town long-term. We certainly had an enjoyable time during the four years we were in Moree, but it was remote and not the sort of place Sharon and I wanted to stay in forever.

So after four years I was offered a promotion and a move to Brisbane. CFL's sales regions were split up into 'districts'. My district had been based around Moree. A number of districts made up a 'zone' and my new position was that of a zone manager.

Late in 1985 I made the move to Brisbane and by this time I had become very career-orientated – aggressively moving towards success.

CFL was now rebranded as Incitec and I worked out of their Pinkenba office. My annual salary was now $30,000. When I accepted the zone manager's role, I recall being asked by a company executive what my wage expectation was, and I nominated $30,000 to which they quickly agreed. I should have asked for more.

Balancing Work and Relationships

I have no doubt that work played a major role in my first marriage breaking up. Sharon and I separated while we were in Moree. It was a case of me being very, very aggressive at my career, totally focussed on it, at the cost of my marriage. I was also doing my accountancy degree, going away on stints at uni and frankly behaving like a bad child. While I was having a great time, the marriage fell away.

So in early 1985, Sharon and I separated. We hadn't quite been married five years. We still got on well but were no longer married. In fact when I was promoted, I didn't want to leave her 'stuck in Moree'. The relocation policy of the company was that they would shift you entirely. So I organised for her to come up to Brisbane with me so that she could at least get out of Moree. Initially we shared a small rental property in Brisbane, but soon after we went our separate ways. I then purchased a unit in Paddington.

So, single times ahead. I was back to making decisions on my own.

The Wisdom of Hindsight

Even though I'd learnt a lot, I had yet to realise how much Dad had influenced me, especially through his harsh discipline. I also had yet to understand 'why' he brought us up the way he did. How could I have known? I was only a child then, viewing the world through a child's eyes.

We have to experience our own life journey to be able to relate to another's reasoning for their actions – and that's if we are smart enough to look back and try to understand. Sadly some never do and therefore never gain the wisdom of hindsight that they could have used for their own life's journey.

While my life was on the up and up, Dad's did not follow a similar trajectory. Soon after I left home in 1978, Mum and Dad sold the Hannaford property and moved down to Guyra, midway between Armidale and Glen Innes on the Northern Tablelands in the New England region of New South Wales. There they bought a sheep farm. Sheep had always been Dad's passion. So when he bought the Guyra property, he was able to live his dream of breeding merino fine wool. He worked that property for thirteen years.

Then in 1982, while finally achieving his life's goals after such hard work, the worst hit us all. Dad was diagnosed with melanoma. This was the start of a very tough time for him and Mum, and the whole family. I remember when the cancer was first discovered, getting the call from the hospital. My mother was on the line, but she couldn't talk from the shock and handed the phone to the nurse to explain the situation to me.

I was still married to Sharon and was about to fly out to New Zealand to meet her there, but instead I went to visit Dad at the Sydney Hospital before I left. He had been transferred to Sydney from Tamworth for immediate surgery. He was distraught. A diagnosis like that will shake anyone.

This was the first time our family had to confront a life-threatening illness. Dad had cancer, a death sentence. We all immediately assumed the worst, as in those days a diagnosis of the big C was always considered to be terminal. So it seemed there would be only one outcome, and it wasn't the one we all wanted for our father.

Perhaps another reason why we all believed the worst-case scenario was because of our upbringing. We always did it tough and thought the worst, for as children we weren't taught to look positively at situations. I had just started at CFL and it wasn't till later in my career that staff personal development training sessions opened my eyes to the reality of 'best-case scenarios' to consider.

So when I visited Dad in Sydney, I wasn't capable of thinking positively, or I thought I wasn't. But I was the eldest son, so I had no choice but to man up and take the lead in the situation and try to be positive for

Mum at least. By default I did step up and became the positive voice in the situation. I recall the night before Dad was due to go into hospital. We went to a pub in Paddington. Unbeknownst to us, it was a gay bar. By the time we realised it, it gave Dad a good laugh. I recall him joking, 'Greg! You might have been able to pick someone up!' At times like that, you grab onto the lighter moments get you through the darker ones.

Unfortunately for Dad, though, he still struggled with a lot of anger and that was the beginning of the end for Mum and Dad as a married couple. As a child I remember a lot of arguments, but it became particularly bad when Dad got sick. He grew angry and antagonistic towards Mum. I sat on the sidelines feeling so sorry for Mum and all that she put up with.

Dad ended up surviving his first battle with cancer after his chemo sessions. But he was very, very sick. He spent quite a bit of time in the Sydney Hospital. He said to me later that his memory of being in hospital was of people dying all around him and thinking he would be next.

But he fought his way through and returned to the farm in Guyra. My uncles and I would go down to the farm for the shearing season and help out. I took time off work. It was about 1987 when Mum and Dad separated and sold the property. Mum moved to Brisbane and Dad went back to Toowoomba.

But Dad's escape from surviving cancer wasn't to be long-lived and he eventually passed away in 1994 after ten years in remission. Although that time was difficult, it was one of incredible understanding and revelation.

He was three weeks away from dying and I clearly recall a moment where I had a sudden epiphany. It was like a lightning bolt had hit me with a flashback from our upbringing. It suddenly occurred to me that all that he had done in his life had just been so that we would not have a life as tough as he had! That is all he wanted for us. That was all he knew. That was the only way he knew how to accomplish it – to be tough on us. It was in those weeks before he died that I forgave him. It was painful. At the time I sought out help from a counsellor and I am glad I did.

I also remember something that Felicite (my second wife) said in the time leading up to Dad's death: 'Don't let him go without saying what you need to say.' She had lost her own dad unexpectedly and her advice was based on her own reflections. I am very pleased I listened to her and made peace with him before he died. I would have regretted it for the rest of my life if I hadn't. And not only did I learn about avoiding future regrets, it also made me thankful for the positive impact Felicite had on my own life and decisions.

Something to Ponder

Has work taken over your life to the detriment of your relationship with yourself and/or those you love?

If your answer is 'yes', do you recognise the potential consequences for yourself and others?

What will it take to make a positive change and bring a better balance to your personal life and work?

CHOICES, CHANGE AND FEARS

Choices, Change and Fears

'Our greatest power is the power of choice; our greatest freedom lies in the exercise of our power of choice.' George W. Curtis

'In most cases, when you say, "I" it is the ego speaking . . . It consists of thought and emotion, a bundle of memories you identify with as "me and my story", of habitual roles you play without knowing it, of collective identifications such as nationality, religion, race, social class, or political allegiance.' Eckhart Tolle

A Podiatrist Realises the Power and Effect of Choice

It was 2000. I'd turned twenty-seven, and by the end of that year, Lisa and I both graduated. We went onto the job market at the same time. Inevitable change was on the horizon. I had been trying to figure out whether I should buy a practice, set up a practice or go work for someone. I had done work experience for a few different people while at uni and one of those was at a practice in Toowoomba – Toowoomba Foot Care Centre. It was owned and run by Joyce Cooper. Joyce epitomised professionalism and she ran a fantastic podiatry practice along with her husband, Ed. Joyce was a great mentor for me during those days of work experience and I knew this was the sort of business I wanted to own.

In my final semester of podiatry at QUT, Joyce called me up and asked if I wanted to come and work in Toowoomba. I had enjoyed my work experience time with Joyce, but there was no way I wanted to live there. Toowoomba, in my eyes then, was a country town. I had mates from Toowoomba and when we would go there it was a surreal experience. Everything seemed so slow, nothing was happening and I couldn't believe my mates could actually live there. So for her to say, 'Come to Toowoomba', I thought, 'No way!'

But Joyce is a smart businesswoman and not easily deterred. She said: 'Well, what if we gave you first option to buy the freehold which includes our house, the practice and the business within two to three years of you graduating?' Suddenly Toowoomba looked slightly more attractive. So we started talking more and more about the proposition and she started to add more flesh to the bone. My starting salary would be $40,000 a year plus super, which in 2001 was a nice starting wage – certainly better than the bottle shops.

But wait. There was more! She promised that after I had been there six months I could start on 40% of billings and then go to 45% after another six months and up to 50% after another six months. And after about three years, I could buy the whole practice for what she promised would be a very reasonable rate.

Excited, I went to Lisa and I told her of this fantastic opportunity and asked her: 'Do you want to do this?' Her answer was a flat 'No'. She did not want to leave Brisbane. I pressed her about how great a deal this was and asked about our alternatives. But Lisa just wasn't interested.

It was at this stage that it crystallised what I had known for a long time – we didn't have a future together. So we fought and fought and fought, and I remember saying: 'Well, I am accepting this job. I think it can really set us up. It is up to you what we do from here.'

But she said: 'No, I am not going.'

Sliding Doors

With that, a couple of decisions were made for me. It was another one of those sliding door moments. I made the decision to leave Lisa – which also meant leaving Ana and that was incredibly tough. I packed up my stuff, moved to Toowoomba, rented a small unit and started my podiatry career.

The fact that my career path was set, albeit in Toowoomba, was fantastic, but the fact that it wouldn't include Ana on a day-to-day basis hit hard. I became the 'every other weekend Dad'. For the first few years after we separated, I would come down every other Friday afternoon and pick Ana up and either take her back to Toowoomba or, more often than not, stay in Brisbane to see Mum and Dad and spend the weekend with her.

At that stage, Lisa and I were not getting on well. We both resented each other. I never fought for custody of Ana. I was probably a bit too selfish to do and did not see myself as being capable. I was still behaving like a child in many ways. I was a very late developer emotionally and I was well into my 30s before I gained any essence of maturity.

But Lisa, for all our disagreements, is a terrific mum. We have a better relationship now than we have ever had before. We respect each other for our differences. At the end of the day, we were both really young then. We did the best we could in the situation. There were things we both did and said that we would like to take back. And I shoulder most of the blame for the problems we had back then. I wasn't an easy person to be around. I was volatile, emotional and selfish.

Overall, I have a massive amount of respect for Lisa. Particularly the way that, as a mum, she managed to not only complete her degree but excel. She has a terrific work ethic. After uni, as she intended, she started on a locum career with a baby, by herself. She then worked at a practice and then bought a practice. She is a pretty incredible woman. She would never take help or assistance from anyone. She is very, very self-sufficient. She has some great qualities – a lot of character. I will always have a huge amount of respect for her and am thankful she raised such a wonderful young lady. It couldn't have been easy.

For me, one of my proudest achievements is my relationship with Ana. Although it was every second weekend, alternate Christmases and a week here and there for holidays, I cherished that time with Ana and can't recall ever missing a weekend. And now Ana and I have a great relationship. She was just my little mate and we did everything together.

Back then, none of my friends or associates had children and so Ana came with me to almost everything, and everyone got to know her really, really well. She was just an amazing little girl. And at that stage, I wore three hats. I was a podiatrist, part-time dad and part-time party-goer who lived it up like he was never going to party again. I have always been pretty social and for a while there I thought it was integral to my DNA, that I needed to socialise that much. When I went to Toowoomba, it was almost like, 'Hey, I'm back. Let's party.' So I juggled those three hats for a couple of years.

Several years later, Lisa married Anthony, a pilot. She had flagged at the time that they might have to move overseas for Anthony's work. At that stage, I felt very uncomfortable about such a move. It was off the table for a while, but then in 2011 she called me and said Anthony had been offered a position in Hong Kong, they wanted to move there and would I let them take Ana?

I agonised over that for a long period of time and it came down to me having to admit what was best for Ana. I would miss her a lot but knew it would be selfish not to let her go – what an amazing opportunity. So I agreed. And so now, four times a year Ana comes home and we get alternate Christmases together. But it has been tough because I have missed out on so much of her growing up – the school concerts, sport, all the little accomplishments and challenges and the big ones too.

She was twelve when she went to Hong Kong and she is seventeen now. She attends the Australian International School and has turned into an amazing young lady. I am very, very proud of what she has done. She is the school captain there now. She has always been a delight (barring those sleepless nights when she was a baby). She really is a special girl.

I believe the experience that Lisa and I have been through also shaped Ana into a capable, independent young lady. She is planning on coming back to Australia for university – to the University of Queensland. So she will be just down the road again and I am really looking forward to that.

Fear vs Opportunity

As far as starting work with Joyce, my first day I felt sick to my stomach. It was Monday, 18 December 2000, and I will never forget it. The previous day I had an enormous argument with Lisa and that was still festering in my mind. Then, on that first day, I had a full book of patients. Historically, I have suffered terribly with nerves and anxiety. I can handle it well now, as it is something that I have worked on it quite a bit. But that day I was almost white with fear. So many things raced through my mind. Then my very first patient walked in.

I sat there thinking, 'This person knows I am not qualified to do this'. But then we started talking. He was a patient who had been to the practice before, and I think he may have sensed my anxiety. He asked how long had I been doing this. And I replied that I had been working on feet for three years – which was true. In my second year at uni, I started working on people's feet.

That was like a self-affirmation. I started to feel at ease and with each patient I felt better. At the end of that day, I recall thinking: 'Well, that was stressful.' We used to see three or four patients in a day at uni, and I saw sixteen in my first day at work.

Fortunately, there were support mechanisms. Joyce was next door and Ed was on reception with another lady. Honestly, I would have preferred to have been eased into things a bit more, but it was sink or swim. So I jumped in and swam like hell. I also soon realised I was well equipped to do what I was doing. But it was a very, very steep learning curve.

The timing was perfect for Joyce – the owner – and I. She was at the end of her career. She wanted to get out. She saw me as a young bloke she could groom. It just so happened I was also looking for that same opportunity. Her and Ed ran a great operation. They were excellent, supportive role models who taught me a heck of a lot about running a good business and being a good doctor.

We became close friends and colleagues. I think they did everything they could to help me grow into the role. They wanted me to meet a nice girl, get married and stay in Toowoomba. I fought that for a long time. As soon as I had an opportunity, I would escape to Brisbane or the Gold Coast.

Ed and I got on very well. Many Friday nights we'd go out for dinner and then stay on for a few drinks and talk about the possibility of me taking over the practice. Their timeframe was in two or three years and they were giving me the first option to buy. I enjoyed talking through scenarios with Ed, and we even spoke about me being able to pay off my investment in the practice in just a couple of years.

I really started to get excited. At the same time, I was making more money than I thought I ever would. I was even able to adjust my shifts – work longer hours Monday through Thursday and then have every Friday off. So that meant I could get down to Brisbane Thursday night and pick Ana up. Everything was working out well. I was learning a great deal from Joyce. She was a really hard worker, super professional, and I was getting more and more excited about the prospect of buying the practice.

As the opportunity appeared to be getting closer, I knew it was time to talk money and ask them exactly how much they wanted. Included in their offer was their house on the corner, which had recently been renovated and was quite nice. Then there was the business premises next door to the house and then of course the business itself. Their asking price was $420,000 for all of it. I thought that was a very fair price considering the business was turning over about $300,000 a year and they ran a very lean operation so they made a good profit.

I was pumped. I had spent eight years of my life studying to complete two degrees and finally here I was about to sink my teeth into a business, a really good practice in an area that was underserviced. The only negative for me was . . . Toowoomba. I kept fighting the idea of living there long term.

I recall one of my mates saying: 'You are not truly going to be happy until you actually accept Toowoomba as your home.' The thing was, I just wanted to be at the Gold Coast all the time. But over time, when I did make that psychological shift, I started to enjoy things a lot more in Toowoomba.

Risk vs Desire

When it came time to buy the practice, I had to find $420,000. I had no experience with banks or loans or any of those things. I had no money, no savings. I spent every cent I earned. And I had no track record of note in the eyes of the financial institutions. So it may have come as a surprise to me, but to few others, when every bank I approached said: 'No!' I ended up asking Mum and Dad for some advice – not money. Mum said I should talk to Nana (Joy).

You see, Nana and Pa had been very shrewd investors and had done quite well with their different businesses and properties. All I was after was the deposit of $80,000. Mum suggested that the deal I put to Nana would be for me to ask for the loan and to pay her back at an interest rate better than the cash rate.

I still remember the conversation with Nana at her unit on the Gold Coast. She was no 'soft touch'. She was initially a little reticent. She insisted that I lay out the entire purchase plan, the figures for the business, everything. She explained that Pa and she had worked far too hard for her to lose their money at their age. Of course, I understood completely and the last thing I would have wanted was to cause her any stress.

But I also knew it was a great deal and that Nana was probably my last chance. What really convinced her was the fact that there were two properties involved so if things didn't go to plan, there were still assets to sell. She had seen how hard I had worked during that time and saw the value in the business itself. I think that was comforting for her.

We agreed on an interest rate of 5%. We didn't actually sign anything and the deal was sealed with a big 'thank-you' hug and a kiss on the cheek. I remain eternally grateful to Nana for having faith in me and giving me a chance. Of course each year I make my repayments to Nana and she is happy because, as she tells me, it is better than the interest the banks would offer. Plus she's helping me.

Nana is 90 now (still fit as a fiddle) and she keeps track of the loan and how much I still owe. I just ask her 'when' and 'how much'. It's a great arrangement still for us both. Remembering that the cash rate is now below 2%, Nana is doing quite well, thank you very much.

So with Nana's money I was able to get the loan required. The sale of the business went through and on July 1, 2004, I officially took over as the owner of Toowoomba Foot Care Centre. I was so incredibly happy, I was bursting at the seams. Joyce and Ed ran the business well, but there were so many areas where I believed I could make things even better. I remember the weekend before I took over, I was just elated.

From Fear to Empowerment

This was one of the most exciting times of my life. I remember walking in at 6.30am on Monday, seeing my first patient at 7am and my last patient at 5.45pm. I went home that night and thought: 'Nothing has changed except now I am trying to figure out the business as well!' But Joyce and Ed continued to teach me. We agreed that they would both stay on for a period. And Ed helpfully showed me the bookkeeping side of the business.

I think we had initially agreed that Joyce and Ed would stay on for about eighteen months. But eventually we all realised that was probably too long. I told Ed that the practice was never really going to be my business until I phased them out. So I employed a fulltime admin person and Ed stopped working at the practice. What I didn't predict was that as a result, a lot of the support I was getting dried up as well. And unfortunately my working relationship with Joyce started to sour. Joyce is an absolute perfectionist and I am not so much. This caused a deal of friction.

Some of the things I was doing with the business Joyce struggled with. She would often kick up a fuss and was reluctant to embrace the changes that I wanted to make. We began butting heads with our different points of view. There is no doubt I was a bit of an upstart in a lot of ways.

I had spent four years learning how to be a podiatrist and then I was arrogant enough to think I could just pick up how to run a business. The reality was that I didn't know what I was doing and I made a lot of stupid decisions.

In terms of a person running a podiatry practice, Joyce was the ultimate professional and an over-achiever in a lot of ways. She started off as a nurse but went back to university, successfully studied podiatry, worked for another practice in Toowoomba and within a very short period of time, set up her own practice and established herself as the paramount podiatrist in the area.

Joyce is a classy, elegant lady. She was probably in her late 50s, early 60s when I met her, and her attention to detail and expectations were at a high standard. I have no doubt my ego played a role in the souring of our relationship for a period. Everyone used to always talk about how great Joyce was. And to be honest, she was great and deserved that respect, but it really bothered me.

So, I worked incredibly hard to establish myself. I worked hard to make patients my own and have them respect me. I remember one of my early highlights being a referral coming in with my name on it. I saw it as a challenge to remove myself from Joyce's immense shadow. Once I took over the practice, I went out of my way to put my own stamp on how we operated and make the practice my own.

The Pitfalls of Ego

I was arrogant enough to think I could just buy a business and nail it. I really didn't have much of an idea. So I leaned on Joyce as much as I could. But I was getting frustrated with her and I had the perception that she was still trying to control things. Obviously this was her baby. She watched me take over and struggled when things did not meet her expectations. A classic example occurred one Christmas-New Year's break, when annually we closed the practice for several days.

This particular year, however, I had not arranged gardeners or cleaners to come in before we re-opened. Joyce came back and ripped into me because of how untidy the whole place was. 'I just can't work in a place like this,' I remember her saying. So, of course, that got my back up. We had a number of similar spats. I changed our pricing structure. I brought in some new orthotic manufacturing technology. These were all valid initiatives in my mind, but Joyce didn't agree. She struggled letting go and I struggled with her not letting go.

Subsequently, Joyce quit and retired earlier than we had planned. It had been coming for a while. It was sad, as we had been close. But it was also inevitable. She had her views on how a business should be run, and I had mine, but now the terms had changed. I was the owner.

There was a clash of egos. I was just focussed on taking the business in my direction and she was no doubt hurt by some of the changes. It was an unfortunate parting. There is no doubt that I didn't fully appreciate what she had allowed me to purchase and the opportunity she had given me.

Over the years we have mended those fences to a degree and we now have an amicable relationship. We still meet for dinner every now and again. I have told them how appreciative I am of the opportunity they gave me and what a fantastic practice they had created. I was glad they were able to come to the opening of my new practice in 2015, and I was able to publicly thank them for their support and the opportunity they provided.

A Coach Realises the Power and Effect of Choice

So, I was twenty-seven, single, highly paid and in my own unit in Brisbane. I had a ball. My early success in business had also made me very confident, very career-oriented and very focussed. To be zone manager so young was a reasonable feat and I was becoming very full of my own confidence. I was bulletproof. And I did well in that new role. We achieved quite a few good things and that resulted in another promotion about two years after moving to Brisbane, which is when I ended up back in Toowoomba.

As zone manager in Brisbane, my territory was coastal – east of the dividing range. It stretched north to Nambour and south to just north of Coffs Harbour. We serviced principally cane, horticulture and some small crops. I had a whole team of salespeople under me. I think I had six reps and there were a couple of agronomists, although they didn't report directly to me.

Within my team there were a couple of guys who were considerably older than I. Our guy in Lismore was in his fifties and I was only twenty-seven. That was challenging and generated some negativity from these older salespeople. So I worked to build a positive relationship with these guys. I just used some of the skills that I had learned in Moree. I realised that these guys would be somewhat hesitant and potentially would resist me as a young buck coming into their territory above them. But I brought with me some credibility with what I had already achieved – the reason why I had been given the promotion. So what I had to prove to them was that I had their interests at heart. This all took time and effort.

Again, what worked in my favour was that I had come from the land. Also, I realised early the importance of family in staff relationships. I made sure I included their families, learned all of their wives' names, and got to know their children. I would also spend a lot of my time out on the road with the sales reps.

Even though I was based in Brisbane, I went out every month. More than half my time was spent on the road with these guys. And I would be out doing sales calls with them and meeting with their distributors. So I got to know them all and the various business and family relationships. Of course, you can't make everyone happy all the time. For example, not all of our distributors were happy people. They all wanted more money and those negotiations were part of the deal.

I worked hard but partied hard as well, especially when I was out on the road. In Moree the culture was very much, 'Okay, it's the end of the week. Time to party all night!' It was a town of a lot of young people just like me. They weren't necessarily locals and so we tended to group together and have a lot of fun. It was a similar story in Brisbane, when I was single again. However in Brisbane I also decided to get back into shape and spent a lot of time at the gym. So I worked hard but had a lively social life as well.

Do What It Takes

I was only based in Brisbane for about two years, 1986 and 1987, as I moved to Toowoomba before the 1988 Brisbane Expo. All this time I continued with my study and I graduated in 1989. My degree helped me enormously. I attribute a lot of my early career success to the skills and education I was getting through that study process. It taught me to be resourceful, because when you're doing external studies, you have to get creative. You can't just cram it.

You have got to actually work through problems and to do things you wouldn't normally do. Like get up at 4am or know where to go to try to find something. There was no library, no Internet. I had to think well ahead of time in order to get books out of the Armidale Library, for example, and have them mailed to me.

My degree also taught me to approach the sales process analytically. Rather than merely reading the numbers, I learned to ask the right kind of questions to increase sales or get salespeople motivated. What are you really looking for? You would see symptoms of something and the study I had done in accounting gave me the resourcefulness to dig deeper. Of course I was never motivated to become an accountant. It was more about just getting a degree. As it turned out, this particular degree has been helpful to me all the way through my work life.

So, by 1988 I was back in Toowoomba and again I received a promotion. Districts were placed in zones and zones into 'regions'. I was now a regional manager. My region went north to Clermont in central Queensland, south to Bourke and Dubbo and west of the range. That is when I got my pilot's licence.

My elevation to Regional Manager, based in Toowoomba, was quite a senior appointment for somebody my age – I was twenty-eight at the time. It came about because the person in that position was retiring and they saw fit to put me into the role. It was a huge acknowledgement for the work I had been doing. No doubt there were other people in the running for that position, and I did not necessarily think I would be handed that role. In fact, I was potentially in the frame for two roles.

One was in Mackay and the other in Toowoomba. Both were similar positions, but Mackay was the more junior role – a regional manager's position, just not in as a key region as Toowoomba was. I was engaged to be married at the time, and Felicite and I were living in Brisbane. So here I was once more, making decisions for myself that also involved consideration for another.

I commuted to Toowoomba and Felicite had a job in Brisbane. I recall her not being all that keen on Mackay, purely for geographical reasons. She had just shifted up from Sydney after Sharon and I finalised our divorce. Then all of a sudden, almost the moment she arrived, I said, 'By the way, we could be going to Mackay or we could be going to Toowoomba.' So that didn't go down well. Her preference was Toowoomba because it was closer to her family.

I have no doubt the promotion to regional manager at CFL was a direct result of my work ethic. I always worked very hard. I also have no doubt this was a positive result from what was instilled in me when I was a child, and because I lived with my parents and watching them do the same. I was always enthusiastic and ambitious.

When I was called in and offered the Toowoomba position, I was humbled and relieved it was Toowoomba and not Mackay. I am not sure how Felicite would have handled Mackay – it's a long way away and so much more humid than the southern part of the state. But I would have taken either position because both were a step up from what I was doing.

Familiar Territory – New Challenges, New Fears

So the promotion to Toowoomba as regional manager was great news, but once again I was in a familiar and slightly challenging position. I was a young man in a role surrounded by many older, and some sceptical, people. So I had to earn people's trust. Under me were at least fifty people including a sales team and a distribution team. And it was quite a big region as well. It took in northern NSW right up to central Queensland.

So gaining respect from everyone meant a lot of travel to get face-to-face not only with our own staff but also our dealers. The dealers were business people who were obviously looking after their own businesses and were keen to get the best arrangements they could, and so there was no surprise that they viewed this new young chap with a degree of scepticism.

But, as I said earlier, this was not new territory for me. I think for most of my life there has always been a new challenge that I have wanted to pursue, always trying to prove that 'I can do it' – to myself but also to my dad. My upbringing was about wanting to be the best at everything and then proving that to my father.

So I think I always wanted my dad's approval. Every time I would have a crack at something, I would go hard at it and largely what I was looking for, subconsciously perhaps, was my father's acknowledgment – which I never really got until just before he died. Such a shame I didn't get it all the way through, but that is what it was.

I first met Felicite while in Moree. She was part of the company's office administration team. We became 'an item' a few months before I moved to Brisbane. When I did move north, she chose to go to Sydney instead and at that point we sort of took a bit of a break in our relationship. But after a while we reconnected again and she shifted up to Brisbane.

Soon after she arrived, I was working in Toowoomba and staying in a motel there, while Felicite worked in Brisbane for a property developer. Within a very short time, we decided to get married on 14 May 1988. For several months leading up to the marriage, I did the Toowoomba commute. Once the wedding and Europe honeymoon were behind us, we relocated to Toowoomba.

Initially the company put us up in a motel, which was more of an apartment than a motel, until we could find something more permanent. We then moved into a flat. I kept the Brisbane unit and rented that out. Eventually we bought a block of land in a new development in Toowoomba on the western side of town, on Hamzah Drive in Cotswold Hills, and decided to build. A bit of advice to newlyweds – building a new home is not a good way to start a marriage.

It was stressful, but Felicite managed the situation well. We moved into our new house on Christmas Eve 1988. So, as I said, Felicite got things done, which is her style. While she had a little trouble finding work, she soon found a job doing the books for an earthmoving business.

My new position with Incitec was challenging, but I loved every minute of it. I thrived in the newness of it all, getting around the whole region and helping people. Some of the people who were reporting to me were much older than I was. So gaining their trust was, again, a challenge that I relished. However as a couple of years ticked by, for the first time in my work career, I began to feel frustrated by certain elements of what I was involved in.

There were a lot of politics in managing my role, especially in obtaining the funding my region needed to continue to be efficient. My skills were stretched as I had to put business cases together that went through to the board level and involved a lot of money. The biggest project I ever put forward was a $10 million new facility project. I had to draw on a lot of skills that I hadn't really used much before, then add in even more politics.

And then, of course, because we were a publicly listed company, there were shareholders and pressures around performance. Throw in the odd drought, which of course will force a downturn in sales, and the pressure rose. Constantly I would receive edicts from the top saying, 'You have got to cut your costs' by whatever means possible. And typically that involved reducing staff numbers.

Re-Evaluation

The turning point for me involved one such edict, which outlined that I had to cut my sales staff. I think at the time I had about ten sales people. I was told to halve that number and double the size of their sales regions. One of the people I had to let go was a new guy to the team who had been doing really well in North Queensland and had been enticed down to join my team. He was a South African fellow, a family man in his 40s.

I remember sitting across the table from him and telling him the news. The memory is burnt into my brain. He was completely gutted and about three weeks later he suffered a major heart attack. His wife was furious and quite abusive towards me, which was understandable. It felt awful knowing the upheaval I had created in this family. So yes, that absolutely was a turning point for me. It was after that when I started to re-evaluate what I was doing.

This episode happened around 1991, after I had been in the regional manager's position for about three years. In all I was there from 1988 to 1992. And during that time my region was performing very well. We were the senior region and certainly our contribution to the company's profits was significant. We were one of four regions and we were contributing more than half of the profit to the organisation in the agricultural area.

By this stage I was probably earning in the early $60Ks, and for somebody of my age, I felt I was on good money. I had also gained my pilot's licence. It made sense to fly as my region was so big. I joined the local aero club in Toowoomba and rented a plane for a week at a time, allowing me to fly around my area and catch up with everyone. So I would fly to nearby Emerald, where the company also had a rep, and we would do the rounds from there. The furthest location in the south was a little place called Warren, which is near Dubbo, and a very big cotton region. So I used to fly to Warren and then west to Bourke.

The company hierarchy seemed fine with me flying a plane. It was just so practical. So one week of every month, I spent it out in the field with my team. I never crashed a plane. While I did get lost once, that worked out okay. Flying was just something I did. I wouldn't say I was passionate about it or that it was in my blood. Certainly, when you are flying it is exhilarating. You are seeing the world from a different place. You also attain a high level of awareness of everything around you. You ensure all your checks and balances are done.

Like most pilots, I did have a few things go wrong. I haven't had an engine failure, but I did have an engine that did fail on me on landing. I landed all right, but it turned out to be a major problem and the plane could not be fixed for some time, so I had to catch a charter flight back to

Toowoomba. The problem was, I had no way of contacting Felicite – this was before mobile phones – and she worried when I didn't arrive back on schedule.

However that particular plane was my favourite to fly. It was a 'Mooney', of Canadian make. It was very quick with a retractable undercarriage and variable prop so I used to cruise at around 160 knots and get around my region quickly. It was not a big plane. It was described as seating four, but it felt crammed with just two people on board. They are called 'The Porsche' of light aircraft – really quick and slick.

So the longer I worked in the new position, the less fulfilled I became with my work. The further I was removed from the frontline, the more I missed working with clients directly. I had been elevated into a role where suddenly I had to become more of an advocate and representative, squeezed between the top's demands to cut costs and the bottom's needs for respect and support.

And then of course there is dealing with people's personalities. And finally . . . the politics. The person I reported to was a highly political person. He was all about positioning and getting the story right. After a while that started to bother me. I felt like some of my authenticity was being lost. I found that what I enjoyed most – actually helping people, giving people a chance – I was doing less and less of.

Two instances stand out as perfect examples. Both involve people I interviewed for positions with Incitec. The first was another South African who had migrated to Australia with his family. He was an older guy and, to be honest, on paper and at the interview, wouldn't have been the person that I automatically would have given the sales job to. There were other candidates who probably sat in front.

But I remember his interview vividly. He looked me in the eyes and there was a deep sincerity about the guy. He said: 'Greg, you know what, I really need this job. I will not fail you because I cannot fail. I have brought my whole family here and I am in a totally new country. I cannot fail and I will give you my absolute best.' So I put his name forward and he was given the position. That guy now has a very senior position in that company. He is still there and he is still performing really well and he has made a real career out of it.

The other example was when a Kiwi chap turned up for a job interview. The process went well and he was a great candidate. I had decided towards the end of the interview that he was 'a keeper'. As we were finishing up, he asked me if there were any other jobs going because he had a mate who had also just arrived from New Zealand and was also looking for a job. He explained that the mate had not applied for the Incitec position because they had decided they would not both go for the same job. I said that I would be happy to have a chat with him if he put in an application. However, not to let a chance go by, the Kiwi said: 'He's outside in the car if you want to chat now.' I thought, 'Why not?'

So, the mate rolled in wearing shorts, thongs and a singlet – not the way you would normally rock up to an interview. But he presented really well and was enthusiastic. So I put both men forward and they both ended up getting a role. In fact both ended up working with me. And again, that guy who turned up in the singlet, shorts and thongs is still at the company and in a very senior role and doing well. Those are a couple of really fond memories. Those were the things I enjoyed doing. And then there were the other parts of the job that concerned me.

The catalyst to me leaving Incitec was actually the fact that my dad was in Toowoomba, semi-retired and looking for something to do. He just couldn't sit still. For a number of years, he had been questioning my career. 'Why build other people's companies and other people's stuff? Why don't you do it for yourself?' he'd say.

He had been self-employed all his life and he really struggled to understand the ethos of working for someone else. He didn't get the whole corporate thing. When my ten-year anniversary at Incitec came and went, I thought more and more about what I was doing and what I wanted to do. I was in my early 30s, but what did I want to do with the rest of my life?

I had been very successful with Incitec and my ego was telling me that I was invincible, there was nothing I couldn't do. The incident with the employee who had suffered the heart attack was also playing on my mind. I didn't want to have that responsibility. So I started searching for a business to buy. Something that Dad and I could be involved in together. I evaluated a few different options and made decisions and choices that, once again, had a massive impact on my own life and those of others, delivering yet even more self-learning in many ways.

This was another momentous time of huge self-realisation. I actually enjoyed working at the 'coal face' and my opinion of sales had changed from hating it to loving it. I realised it was all about my own negative perception of sales from way back. But it became a very positive experience. I also reflected a lot on that employee I'd let go. Would he have had the heart attack if the work pressures I had been party to hadn't happened? Did I contribute to his stress? It weighed on me heavily and I experienced a lot of guilt thinking that I may well have, even though I wasn't to know for sure.

Dad had also been pressuring me to do something for myself and get away from sales – white collar work. In addition to his desire for me to work for myself, he believed I didn't have a 'real job' in sales. He had always believed that white collar work wasn't 'real work' and that blue collar was 'true work'. He couldn't understand and wouldn't look at it any other way because he had only known what he had lived. So he pushed me to build a business for myself to get away from 'sales' and I succumbed to the pressure. What definitely helped with that decision was my own guilt and stress regarding the heart attack.

So I left the company and jumped ship to start in business. Did I jump for the wrong reasons? Maybe. Maybe not. Yet another period of deeper learning for me, and even in hindsight I will never know. I would probably not be doing what I am now at very least. A life-changing decision, taking another path for a different future, and there were future lessons ahead. A sliding door moment?

Something to Ponder

Have you made choices and decisions which you felt were intuitively wrong at the time, but made them anyway?

If so, what was the outcome of those choices, and what steps did you take to move forward?

If you are struggling with a decision right now, perhaps ask yourself – what is the worst that can happen? And what is the best that can happen?

TAKING
RISKS

Taking Risks

'Your greatest gift lies beyond the door named fear.' Sufi saying

'Wisdom is knowing what to do next, skill is knowing how to do it, and virtue is doing it.' David S. Jordan

A Podiatrist Puts It All on the Line

So I am finally on my own, with my very own practice all to myself, in September 2005. With Joyce and Ed now off the scene, I barrelled in as hard as I could to try to get the practice moving in the direction I wanted. However, I soon realised owning a business is not all that it is cracked up to be and being an employee is actually a pretty good life – paid holidays, paid superannuation, etc. Oh yes, I had all this money coming in, but it was going out just as quickly. There is no doubt I had an unrealistic expectation on the amount of responsibility, the lack of autonomy and the amount of stress involved in owning a business.

Early on I went to my accountant and he showed me all the outgoings, including of course, tax. I said to him: 'There has got to be a better way.' But he explained in very basic terms some business principles, including that until I had more than two people working for me, I would remain in the top tax bracket. This is when I learnt the term 'personal exertion'.

So I came away with the mindset that I needed another podiatrist as soon as possible. Up until then, there had always been just the two podiatrists – initially, Joyce and me, and then me as the boss. So, after my 'tax update', and while Joyce was still working at the practice, I employed Sam who was straight out of uni, a new graduate like me, but who had a bit more life experience. And when Joyce indicated she wanted to resign, I hired Anne-Maree. Both Sam and Anne-Maree have been with me for ten years.

Through this period, the podiatry side of things was going quite well. Sam, like me, had a very, very basic induction into the practice. He came in a few days before starting and was told: 'This is what the practice looks like, this is what we do. Good luck, you'll be fine.' He hit the ground running and did well. It was a similar scenario for Anne-Maree. We were all working four days, but after a while, because of the workload and building cash flow stress, I moved back up to five days.

My weekends and nights were absorbed with writing work-related correspondence, bookkeeping and managing any HR or IT issues. This was all the back-end stuff that I hadn't considered before buying the practice, and I had very little working knowledge in this area at all. I had approached the business from a naïve perspective. On the other hand, I also really didn't appreciate my position, how good I had it and that I just needed to be conservative.

I was always looking for an easier way. I sought financial advice, again, thinking there had to be a better way to make money. But the advice was always: 'Look, don't do anything crazy; just reduce your debt. Hit your debt! Hit your debt.' And, of course, that is exactly what I should have done. But didn't. I just kept trying to get bigger and bigger and bigger, as opposed to consolidating what I had. It was just impatience and a lack of education around what the smart approach would have been. I thought that the only way to reduce my mounting financial stress was to grow. I obsessed over how to grow our revenue.

I was working hard; there were lots of patients and payments coming in. But I didn't understand the concept that the business's money wasn't my money. So if I needed money, I would just take it from the business. Then I was given a rude shock when the accountant sat down and explained that businesses didn't work that way.

I had been busily digging myself into a hole. And it wasn't as if I led a crazy lifestyle. It was just poor planning and financial control – no money was put aside for the taxman. If there was money in my account, I would spend it, usually on new pieces of equipment for the practice. One of my first significant purchases a $90,000 orthotic manufacturing machine, which at the time was far too extravagant for our needs. In retrospect, it was one of the best things I ever did for our patients, but the impact on my cash flow in the early years was significant.

Glass Ceilings

Subsequently, the pressure on me continued to mount. Now I read a lot and have become familiar with a line a thinking that I believe applied to me then at that stage of my journey. And here it is:

Many of us have a perceived 'limiting factor', or a subconscious glass ceiling for what we believe is possible for us as far as success, money, love and happiness is concerned. And as we approach that glass ceiling, we find a way to subconsciously sabotage actually reaching it. That has been the recurring theme throughout my life. I had a business that I never thought I would have. I was making more money than I ever thought I would. I had a great opportunity and a great life, but I continually did my best to sabotage it, whether it be through my lifestyle, the decisions I made or spending money on whatever. It was like the resistance in my head thought, 'Things are going really well. How can I bugger this up?'

A real positive for me around this time in Toowoomba was that my friendship group included several people who also owned their own businesses. Some were highly successful. I was given a good piece of advice early on from a mate of mine, Clinton, who was a prosperous entrepreneur. He told me that, at the very least, I had to employ a bookkeeper. It was good advice, but, as I was to find out soon, that was just the tip of the iceberg of advice that I required.

So he connected me with his bookkeeper and it was one of the best decisions I ever made. That step, so basic and simple, took an enormous weight off my shoulders. Up until then I was doing all the bookwork and through my inexperience, it took up a huge amount of my time. There were bigger problems in my business, though, in the form of a complete lack of training and structure. When someone quit or took sick, it created panic. How would we replace that person? I had no idea. Consequently, I rarely took time off – I couldn't.

Even though I had two podiatrists working for me, I was still billing more than 50% of the revenue. So the breaks I took were very short and infrequent. And I hated Christmas. Christmas meant I had to go see Lisa, Ana's mum, which invariably would lead to an argument and stress. But also, it meant the business was closed across the Christmas/New Year break, so no money was coming in, yet the bills still piled up. My only solution to these dramas was to just keep growing.

Since then, I have often referred to revenue as being porn for business people – I just got obsessed with growth. I started looking for lots of different opportunities. I started a small satellite clinic in Gatton, a small town about thirty minutes away. I said 'yes' to another opportunity in Warwick, another small town forty-five minutes away. And who was the one driving to service these locations? Yours truly.

The Gatton and Warwick clinics would each open just one day a fortnight. With time and hard work, these grew to weekly, then a few times a week and then eventually we set up a fulltime clinic in Warwick. Wherever we went, we were busy. There was no marketing needed, just word of mouth.

I continued to say 'yes' to any opportunity that arose. I thought at the time that all my glass ceilings had been broken by now and were non-existent. At the time it may have felt that way, but I still encounter this self-sabotage at times right up to today. It's a continuing challenge that one day I hope to overcome.

Soon we were also going to Dalby. This of course required me to hire more staff. The trouble was, I was expanding without getting the central business working properly. I just kept stretching the rubber band. We were busy, I employed more staff, but still I couldn't take a holiday. And the cash flow was still really, really tight. The money just seemed to disappear.

I always stressed about bills, stressed about wages, stressed about running the business and trying to keep the team happy. I was also living a slightly excessive life. I used to drink more than I should, smoke more than I should and I wasn't looking after myself. While I didn't know it at the time, I was driving myself straight off a cliff. Something had to change.

Realising Desperation

I remember sitting in my clinic on a Saturday morning, alone, looking at the gaps in the diary for the following week, looking at the wages that were due the following Thursday, looking at the bills in my in-tray and looking at my bank account in overdraft. I could feel tears welling in my eyes. I had no idea how I was going to be able to pay wages. The possibility (make that the probability) of letting someone go would have broken my heart. These guys and girls had put their trust and faith in me and I was letting them down. I realised I was failing. I was failing my staff and ultimately, I was failing our patients. My ego completely shattered. Now I am not sure if I had depression at this stage, but I must have been pretty close. These were dark times.

Within a short time of taking over the practice, I had paid off a slice of my original debt, but instead of consolidating, I bought shares. In fact I always found something else to pour money into. Then the good old GFC came around and that wiped me of about $400,000. A substantial amount of this was borrowed money too. I was in a lot of trouble. I just kept finding ways to lose money – ramming myself against that glass ceiling. So, I remember that Saturday morning vividly. The recurring thought was: 'How the hell can I get more money in here?'

I sat there thinking:

What aren't we doing?

What could we be doing extra?

What am I missing?

A Coach Puts It All on the Line

It was in my early thirties that I evaluated a few different options after reviewing my role and future at Incitec. I had decided to take the risk to do something different and work for myself, and with Dad. We ended up buying a car rental firm together and created a partnership with a family who already operated the business – a well-known car hire franchise.

I had decided to stay at work at Incitec right through until we had become the official partners at the rental firm, so for a while I was juggling my old job with all the stresses of taking up the new role. I had given my notice at Incitec and I recall the day we actually settled on the car rental firm. I was in a meeting with my team at Incitec in Toowoomba in one of the meeting rooms.

A call came through for me, which was a bit odd because I normally asked for all calls to be held and we would take them in the break. But the office administration lady said: 'You need to take this call.' The caller informed me that on the day we were buying into the franchise, the franchisor had just appointed a receiver and manager (the step before an indebted company is liquidated).

My life dropped into chaos. I was still in the meeting, actually leading the meeting, and yet my future plans had been shattered. I remember the confusion. At the time I blocked out the receivership news and thought, 'Okay, I need to deal with this meeting and I need to get on with it.' I also had a terrible feeling in the pit of my stomach, thinking, 'What does this all mean?'

We were a franchise so we weren't the actual franchise company, but we were one of their franchisees. I hoped (thinking positively) that maybe we were removed far enough from the situation so it would not affect us directly. After closing the meeting, I told my office that I had 'received some news' that I needed to go deal with. I met with the new partners at our house at Cotswold Hills. We were trying to work out what the collapse actually meant to us and what we need to do. What it meant was that a business I had just spent $360,000 on was in trouble right from the start.

Strategic Thinking in Troubled Times

So we decided to continue to operate. As franchisees, we were still able to operate, but we were operating under an administrator/receiver. But we needed to rebrand – and quickly. Strategically we felt that because this was the second time our franchisor had gone bust, their (and therefore our) name was tainted, thus compromising our future business growth. We chose to switch to another car hire franchisor that was an emerging rental car business at the time.

This was all happening in early 1992. Later I received legal advice that suggested that maybe there had been a breach of contract and we could have withdrawn from the purchase of the rental car business, but that was not advice I had at the time. The partnership breakdown was that of the half of the business that 'we' owned: Felicite and myself had two-thirds and Dad owned one-third. I had also left Incitec, so that safety blanket had disappeared.

There was so much I learned out of that experience. They are lessons that I carry forward to today, but when I went into that business, it was with total naïveté. I was supposed to be invincible. Whatever I touched turned to gold. On paper the car rental business looked good. There were good profit margins. All we had to do was get all the good corporate accounts, some regular clients and just keep renting cars.

Now, with the benefit of hindsight, even without the calamity of the collapse of the franchisor, there would have been problems. I was entering a business that I knew nothing about. The reality was that this business venture was really an escape. I felt I had done my time in the corporate world and reached that juncture where I had to make a choice – go down the private business path or the corporate path.

And there was another trigger. Incitec wanted to move me back to Brisbane. They wanted me to take on a role which was a sideways move into a management position in their transport division. The money on offer was around the $60,000 mark, which was what I was already earning. It was all about grooming me for upper management.

It would have meant moving back to Brisbane, which by then Felicite wasn't keen to do. It would have also sent me well down the corporate road, which I think I would have walked successfully. But would I have been happy? Probably not. So I chose a different path.

The lesson here? I think I actually chose the car rental business more as a reason to leave rather than it being the best business to leave to. There was certainly room for me to have done more due diligence and asked far more questions about the business.

Trust and Due Diligence

With the franchise collapse behind us, we launched under our new franchise name in Toowoomba. We should have been off and running – finally. But no. Yet another challenge arose. It wasn't long before we realised that the people we had gone into business with – our partners – were crooks. This was revealed when our bookkeeper came to me one day and said: 'You need to get Felicite in here to have a look at the books.'

At that stage, both Dad and I worked on the premises, and Felicite, a bookkeeper, was working for a legal firm in Toowoomba. Obviously I was a little dumbstruck and asked the bookkeeper what she meant. She told me she 'couldn't say', but we needed to have a closer look at the books. I thought, 'Okay'. Things unravelled from there.

First the partners objected to any such scrutiny. We demanded to see the books, and when that happened, Felicite found that they were embezzling funds. Cheques were being made out to creditors, but the partners were changing the payee's name to their own and then forging my father's signature.

So now we had a situation where the business eked by under financial stress, had one set of partners embezzling funds, yet we were still all working under one roof in a tiny office. The relationship between us and them soured quickly and they started getting angrily antagonistic towards us. This latest revelation came in after owning the business for about three months. It was an impossible situation.

Work until then had been Dad labouring out in the vehicle bay. He was doing a lot of the cleaning, which at his age was the last thing I wanted him to be doing, but he wanted to make a contribution. I was on the road selling, trying to drum up business. We had locations in Brisbane as well as Toowoomba, and I was spending quite a bit of time between the two. But as the theft was revealed, I sought legal advice about how we could work our way out of this.

The advice was that, as a director of the company, I was responsible for what was happening, including the embezzlement. So I had to take court action against the other partners. That is the path we took and at the same time we reported the embezzlement to the CIB. That led to the partners being arrested and put in the watch house. It was a terrible, messy affair. I was thirty-two and totally broke. A low, low point in my life.

The police investigation took some time, most of 1993. While this was going on, Dad became very ill and passed away in February 1994. He woke up one day and his arm was black. He called me up, I came over and he just looked me in the eye and said, 'It's back.' I tried to be positive, but the cancer had returned and it progressed quickly. I have no doubt the drama of the failed business venture played a major role in his death. In fact he died just before the court case, only by a couple of weeks.

Facing Total Failure

When the matter did go to court, both our side and the police thought it would be an open and shut case. It was just so obvious. We had a handwriting expert. The handwriting expert presented at the committal. Clearly Dad's signature had been forged on the cheques. However I had never been to court before and I had to appear as a witness, as did Felicite and others. I started to have fears when, while I was giving evidence, I looked across and the presiding judge was asleep. But when it was over, after two days, we all felt that it went well.

Then the call came through and we were told the judge had thrown the case out because Dad had not been alive to give evidence, to state that the signature on the cheques was not his. It was a devastating blow. I felt guilty that Dad died because of the pressure of this whole affair. Now, even after his death, justice had not been served.

We were left crippled emotionally and financially. We had no business, the franchise had been handed back and the business itself was put into receivership and quickly liquidated. We had to sell our home which we were very proud of. After everything had been sold up, I was not earning an income and still owed $60,000 to the bank. That was it. We were cleaned out.

I went straight to the bank manager – those were the days when you could talk to your bank manager – and explained the situation. I told him: 'The only thing I can say to you is I won't default. I will keep going. I don't want to be bankrupt; I just want to forge ahead.' The bank manager agreed not to force me into bankruptcy. I had to plead with Mum to allow me to use her home as security for the $60,000 debt, something she willingly did, but I felt like such a huge failure for having to put her in that position.

Working Through the Darkest Hours

The one thing I have learnt is that even in the darkest of hours, there is always room for a little light, if you are prepared to look hard enough for it. You just have to keep moving forward. While the court action was going through its machinations, I was at a business function in Toowoomba where a friend of mine asked what I was up to. I explained what was happening and said that I was on the lookout for something to do.

He was starting a financial planning practice, a new practice, in Toowoomba. He was doing this on his own and asked if, since I was an accountant, I would mind coming along to evaluate his work. Obviously my confidence level was at an all-time low at that point, but I thought, 'Well, I need to do something.' So I started moonlighting there. I spent whatever spare time I could actually sitting in his practice. And soon I had clients in front of me again.

Initially I felt guilty and like a total failure. How could I sit in front of these people and offer them financial advice with what was happening to me? I kept thinking: 'If they knew what I'm going through, there is no way in the world they would be sitting across the table listening to my advice'. I had to struggle my way through that. After a while, it started to work.

I wasn't being paid, but as things looked as though they were working, my friend revealed that his business involved two franchises and he offered me one of them. The franchise was trying to get established so there was little cost involved. I agreed. They were relatively new. I thought that if I could survive financially, then I was willing to give it a crack. I didn't want to go back into employment.

Of course, I likely could have returned to Incitec. The managing director said to me as I was leaving that if ever I changed my mind, there would always be a job for me. But my pride wouldn't allow that. I didn't want to go back cap in hand to them and say that I had totally stuffed up and could I have my job back? And to be honest, I am not sure if they would have offered it to me anyway.

I decided to give the new financial planning franchise a real go. I wasn't new to hard work and I had to work hard because they were tough years. Felicite was still working, keeping us afloat. We were renting a place down on the southern side of Toowoomba on five acres and living a hand-to-mouth existence. In fact the rent was difficult to get each week. Felicite kept us afloat through her wage and income from her bookkeeping business.

And I was busily trying to build a business – and my confidence – again. The first couple of years were tough. The area I had been given as a franchise was a country region that was in drought so my clients weren't in a state of confidence. I had to spend a lot of that time building relationships, just as I had done so many times with Consolidated Fertilisers/Incitec. I didn't turn a profit in that business for about two years. It was a struggle. I had to put the suit on, but the person underneath the suit wasn't a very confident person. For a long time, I remained embarrassed. I struggled to get my mindset through that last failure. And of course, throughout my whole life, failing had never been an option.

While I had my financial stresses through this period, Felicite continued to be the major bread-winner. She worked as a bookkeeper for a couple of firms before starting her own bookkeeping business. By looking after the books for small businesses, she generated a reasonable income.

There is no doubt my financial concerns had an impact on both of us and our relationship. But Felicite, she is a fighter. She is a survivor. And through that whole period, she shielded me from a number of stressors. Issues like creditors, personal tax, and our budget she just handled while I had my own concerns.

She was strong, very strong, through that whole period and she held it together for both of us. She was so supportive of me although we had lost everything. And now that I pursued a new franchise opportunity to rebuild what I'd lost, she continued to support me.

The easy thing to do would have been for me to just go and get a job. But I wasn't keen to do that, and she understood. And the fact that she was earning money was crucial because I was starting up a new business that would not turn a dollar for some time.

This whole experience was the absolute low point in my life. My personal esteem had hit rock bottom and my confidence in myself had evaporated.

Something to Ponder

Have you taken risks, either personally or professionally, wondering what might have happened (or not happened) if you hadn't?

Have you thought you failed, then realised it was actually a blessing that contributed to success?

Are you frightened to take any risks, calculated or not, because of a fear of failure? If so, and you have done all your homework and due diligence, why not replace that fear with ecstasy and excitement for your potential success?

FAILURE CONTRIBUTES TO SUCCESS

Failure Contributes to Success

'Life can be found only in the present moment. The past is gone, the future is not yet here, and if we do not go back to ourselves in the present moment, we cannot be in touch with life.' Tich Nhat Hanh Zen Master

'We are generally afraid to become that which we can glimpse in our most perfect moments.' Abraham Maslow

A Podiatrist Recovers

So I had lost a fortune as a result of the GFC result (note: it wasn't the GFC's fault; it was mine), but I knew there must be something we could do that we weren't currently doing. That was the day that I started looking at veterans' health. We were already treating a lot of veterans. And I came up with the concept of foot health checks. We would do an annual screening of all the different areas of foot health you need to look at – whether it be dermatology, biomechanics, footwear, orthotics, or a neurovascular assessment – and we would do this every twelve months, document it all, create a report, go through that with the patient and send it on to their doctor. We would apply this to all of our regular patients. It was a great way to provide proactive health care instead of just sitting back waiting until symptoms present.

This proved a great way of optimising everything we should be doing for our regular patients, plus a great way of communicating with the doctor. The financial result was an extra $30k to $40k a year. This highlighted that although my business model was far from perfect, there was more we could be doing, more ways to add value. I was not prepared to roll over and quit. There were too many people depending on me. I was in dire straits, but finally I had the clarity to sit down and try to figure out a solution.

A Dream Becomes a Nightmare

But my main solution was just to work harder and longer. I just did more and more. I said 'yes' to more and more opportunities without actually stopping and figuring out what the real problem was. I just poured everything I had into the business. The problem was I was burning out. Unfortunately Benson and Hedges and red wine became very good friends of mine. I was highly proficient at systematic sedation. Using alcohol and smokes to escape from the world for a while. I would also look for any opportunity go out, play up, hide behind my mask that everything was okay and forget my troubles for a night. I did this way too much.

My work mindset got to a point where I just wanted to walk away. I was over it all – the long hours, the workload, the stress. The dream had become a nightmare. I hated almost everything about the practice. I wanted to go find something where I didn't have the stress and the pressure. At times I considered selling the practice. But the reality was the business was heavily built around me.

There were no systems, there was no structure. There was nothing really to sell. It was a glorified job, with all the pressures of a business. I couldn't walk away because I had so many people depending on me, especially my staff. They were really good people. They had faith in me. So, I just kept pushing on, putting on a brave face. Remember, I had taken over this rock-solid, thriving business and in just two to three years, I was floundering. Because there had been no proper plan, no direction, no structure, I had carefully built up a house of cards and it wanted to collapse.

I lived with the feeling that everything was imploding around me. I felt like an absolute fraud. I was showing up at work pretending to be this successful guy with a successful clinic. But the reality is I was terrified. I was embarrassed. I was also spending too much money because the cohort I was hanging out with were all very successful, and there is no doubt I tried to keep up with the Joneses in a lot of ways. But, in my heart, none of it felt real. I did my best to stuff up a great business. And it is true that I was an excellent podiatrist. No doubt there are better podiatrists out there, but I had a great way of communicating with patients and I wasn't afraid of working hard.

But that was also part of my problem – I thought hard work alone would fix it all. After all, it had worked for Nana and Pa, and then for Mum and Dad. So I just kept pouring the lighter fluid on the fire, telling myself, 'She'll be all right!' But it wasn't just work that was failing. In my personal life, things weren't going well either. A five-year relationship had ended about this time. I was devastated. My life was a mess.

Admitting Mistakes and Getting Help

It was around this time that a couple of very good mates of mine suggested that I needed some help – some business coaching. As successful businessmen in their own rights, they knew enough about life and business to know that I needed support. These guys were from solid, successful families and they ran prosperous businesses. They were also shrewd businessmen whom I respected immensely. So when they spoke, I listened.

I would often talk to them about business and what was going on in mine. I was also looking at other businesses and franchises, because they would have to be easier than what I was doing. Wouldn't they?

One of my mates set me straight: 'Parso, get your own house in order first before you start chasing other stuff. You can't ride two horses with one ass.' That was one of my patterns – chase something shiny to fix my problems and distract me from what was really going on.

So I looked closer to home and analysed what I could do to improve my current business. As I mentioned earlier, it was suggested that I consider getting a business coach. I had heard about them in the accountancy field, but I wasn't aware of anyone in the health field. I had been exposed to a business coaching firm once before, but to me it sounded very 'cookie cutter' – one slice of advice was supposed to be all things to all businesses.

I felt I needed someone who had experience in health. So the need for coaching started to really make sense to me, but I did nothing about it until that rather raw moment with my mate Troy Morgan, a fellow health professional. He suggested that I meet Greg Gunther. And so I did.

A Coach Recovers

Recovery While Moving Forward

It was 1993. At only thirty-four years old, I was still recovering emotionally and financially from the two car hire failures which all happened within twelve months. I was moving forward and working on the new financial planning franchise. Meanwhile, Felicite and I were approached to join a relatively new network marketing group.

Through my whole life, I'd never been comfortable with network marketing, not in person nor even in concept. We all hear about different network schemes, and this particular one was a breakaway from one of the world's largest network marketing companies at the time, who had products that were quite good.

The motivation for me to join the network marketing group wasn't about making money. I knew from past experience that it is only the very few in the upper echelons of those sorts of schemes who make good money. For me the motivation was the personal development. Network marketing is really hard, but what that area of business does really well is training, especially in personal development.

For example, initially I was sent a book a month specifically on personal development, and to this day I still have many of those books. I diligently made sure I read those books and took their messages on board. I even workshopped for myself a lot of the exercises. That was a turning point for me in my own confidence and esteem – taking on that training, embracing that training.

The company also conducted monthly training evenings that we would attend in Brisbane. Engaging in network marketing means you have to bring on new members and so we had to approach people, essentially making a cold-call. Although I had a history in sales, this was still way outside my comfort zone. Felicite and I weren't involved in that company for long. After about eighteen months, we stepped away.

But that was a time of needed growth. I had much to learn about personal development, and it would have cost me a lot of money to do it. Through the network marketing company, I got it for free. In retrospect I am proud that I did that because it was a smart move. It was about being honest with myself, knowing what I really needed and realising if I couldn't try something like that, then the way forward was going to be a long road. I just needed an injection.

From Failure to Success

So network marketing was happening while I worked with the financial planning franchise. But when we ended the former, I put all my energies back into the franchise. That was really my venture, making a success out of our franchise, and a business that I was fortunate enough to own. By early 1993 I was formally appointed as a 'proper authority', an authorised representative of our financial planning franchisor. I was with that company until 1997. The franchisor went through some ownership changes. One of the attractions of the franchisor when I became involved initially was that it was owned and run by two people and their staff. So it was independent, privately owned.

Then it was bought out by a multi-national company around 1996. I remember at the time thinking, based on my corporate career when Consolidated Fertilisers went through a similar change, the result would not be great. So the pending changes at the financial planning franchise raised red flags early on.

At that point I started to do some of my own business planning, considering how the changes might affect me and what strategies I had at my disposal. It is interesting to look back at that business planning – which I did just recently. Many of the goals I planned, which I did not think would come to fruition, actually did. Within a matter of two to three years, I got my own financial planning licence, established my own business and departed from the franchisor.

The financial planning franchise years were, as always, on a learning curve, necessitating hard work. I travelled a lot, trying to build relationships with potential clients. I had to build a trust with accountants so they would be happy for me to consult with their clients. Some federal legislation passed at that stage that was also helpful to me. It was in relation to superannuation, in particular self-managed superannuation funds. It required every self-managed super fund to have an investment strategy.

Of course there were a lot of accountants who had a large number of clients placing their cash in their self-managed super funds with no investment strategy whatsoever. It presented an opportunity for me to contract myself to go through that process with these people. The major opportunity came to me via a firm in Moree who had a large number of clients, quite wealthy ones, with self-managed super funds who needed an investment strategy. So I camped myself in Moree, working out strategies for heaps of clients.

Past Achievements = Future Rewards

Of course Moree was where I had spent my formative years with Consolidated Fertilizers, and one of the partners in the firm I was now doing investment strategies for was married to a former co-worker from Incitec. So that work came through previous networks – often the case in the business world. My work in Moree did mean a lot of travel. I drove there every fortnight and remained a couple of days, staying with my sister-in-law. Fortunately they had a bungalow-granny flat that allowed me to stay close to town. I was able to work long hours while there for those couple of days.

The attraction for me as a financial advisor was being able to work directly with clients with problems – problems I could help solve through financial planning. Having the accounting degree was a big advantage. I was able to understand people's situations, and our franchisor at the time, like all major dealer groups, provided me with intense training. As an authorised representative, you must keep yourself abreast of all the latest legislation changes and the like.

So I think, while the form was financial planning, my personal motivation for working this job was to see people reach success. I loved being able to take a particular situation that people were in, help them through that and in the process actually set them up and save them a lot of money through clever tax strategies, thus helping them achieve the outcomes they were really looking for. For me the key motivation was seeing people realise dreams they never thought they'd be able to reach.

I felt good about what I was doing. An appointment with a client would last for about two hours and I would think, 'Gosh, where did that time go?' I would be engaged in deep conversation, often very personal and complex. I was working through problems with people. It felt right and it also seemed to come naturally to me. It also helped me gradually erase some of my own personal doubts that had plagued me since the car rental business disaster.

I do remember, in the early days of the financial planning days, sitting across from affluent clients and suppressing the questions I was asking myself: 'How am I possibly qualified to advise these people? If they knew my past, they wouldn't be sitting where they are.' But through the course of time and a couple of accomplishments that I had with people, I rebuilt and my confidence grew. I knew I was providing value. I became what I considered to be a successful financial planner. A helpful advisor.

I don't think I ever achieved the confidence levels I had earlier in my career when I believed I was invincible. However, I am a lot wiser now. I don't kid myself that I know everything. I listen more and ask more questions. Whatever is in front of me I challenge a lot more than I used to. In any situation – whether one presented by a client or by life – I dig deeper below the surface without fear of rejection or conflict. The experience of having a business failure taught me that. Confidence-wise, I am not sure the scars ever totally leave you.

While you might present a solid mask when you are in front of people, there is the thin edge. To this day, people can say something totally innocently that will trigger things in my mind. Once you have tasted failure, the taste will always be there. But certainly by the mid to late 1990s, I was at a point where I knew I was actually doing something of value, which for me meant that I valued myself a lot more. As a result, personal development is something, even to this day, that I still pursue.

Be Real, Be Honest, Be Authentic, Be Credible

It took me at least five years to be able to talk about the business failure. It was something I was embarrassed by and couldn't talk about it. I felt as though I would be judged and certainly in the world of advising, particularly around money, I felt like a fraud for a long time. After five years I was able to open up a little bit more about it and reflect on what I had actually learnt from the experience and be able to talk about those learnings.

As I was advising in the financial planning world, I had a number of business clients whose problems raised red flags with me because of what I had been through. I knew that I needed to warn these people and suggest some things that could be done. So the scars were now a help. That is when I first started getting an interest in broadening my skill sets beyond just financial planning. It was on these few occasions, and I didn't talk about it absolutely freely, that I shared my own personal experience, what had happened and how I had come through that tough time.

It actually gave me a little bit of credibility with these people. Now, many years after the actual event, of course I know I am better at what I do because of those hard times. It was the turning point in my life. Absolutely. Even though it was my darkest hour, it was the time in my life when I learned the most. I often say it – it is a lesson I needed to learn. Had I just kept going on my path the way I was, I am not sure where I would have ended up.

Whereas now, I am more authentic. I don't externalise things so much anymore. I value myself and I try to encourage people to start to look more within themselves rather than out there as their measure of success. It's given me a more wholesome approach to self-evaluation.

I also don't seek the acknowledgement that I used to. For me it used to be so much about what people thought of me. Now that doesn't matter so much; it is more about how I feel about myself. And really, nobody actually needs to acknowledge me. It is nice when it happens, but I don't need it now.

So yes, that whole bitter experience moulded me. I wouldn't be doing what I am doing now, I wouldn't be working with the fantastic people that I am, had it not been for that particular experience. So it was just one of those life experiences that needed to happen to get me where I am today. And it was obviously designed to be that way.

You could look at that whole disaster around the rental car business as just being plain bad luck and that none of it was really my fault. Unfortunately 'shit happens'. We all have those experiences to varying degrees.

Where I am at now, my whole mindset is that I created that situation. I have to take responsibility. Yes, all of the stars aligned for it to turn sour, but if you consider each of the factors that led to that failure, I either allowed it to happen through neglect or caused it to happen through short-sighted decisions. I was the one driving it so I created it, therefore I had to take responsibility for my own decisions, and then work my way through it.

That moment of realisation was the dawning of the way forward for me. I had been 'the victim' for quite some time. But when I could say: 'Hang on a minute. I created that. I have to take responsibility. I need to now take what I need to from it and work my way forward' – that's the moment when I could learn and move on to success.

So it was a lesson I had to have. It is all about choices, and there are consequences to the choices we make, good or bad. I could have made other choices, so it was all up to me in the end.

Keep Moving Forward

So it is 1998, I have my own licence as a financial advisor and I am ready to separate from the franchisor and set up my own practice. However that was easier said than done because it also meant I had to separate away from my good friend, Tim, who gave me the opportunity in the first place. I remember at the time feeling guilty about the situation.

Earlier in our work relationship I had hinted that I'd one day make this move. At that time, I felt that in my ideal world he would accept it. But back then Tim made it very clear that it wasn't a path he wanted to take. In fact, at the time, each of our franchises were doing very well. We were sharing rented premises and so Tim and I decided the logical move was to combine those businesses as one – a partnership. We also added a third partner – Geoff Doyle. So as we moved forward and I had some discussions with Tim about eventually moving away from the franchise company, Geoff was aware of these discussions and he told me he was keen to go in the direction I had indicated.

He didn't want to continue down the franchise path. So he and I started having the midnight conversations about how we could structure our own licence. We even started going through the process of applying to do it. I wrestled with a deep feeling of guilt because we were doing this all behind Tim's back. But there really was no other option. Geoff and I got to the point when we were successful in getting the licence to set up our own financial planning practice and then we had to 'come clean' to Tim.

That was a painful conversation. He reacted how I expected him to. He was furious. I just had to steel myself for that particular reaction. I sat down with him, just he and I in the room, and I said to him: 'Mate, just put yourself in my shoes. Do you want me to just go with you and be party to something I don't believe in, which means you have got a business partner here who is not on board? Or do you want us to be truthful and remain friends, but take different paths?'

The result, unfortunately, is that we were never close friends again after that. I can certainly have a coffee with him or even have a meal with him, but there is always that little bit of distance. With the benefit of hindsight, I should have kept my franchise separate. And unfortunately we had to work behind Tim's back. He had made it very clear early on that that wasn't a path he wanted to take. Geoff and I didn't want to get to a 'majority votes' scenario for the partnership's future.

From my experience, you are either in or you are out. You can't drag people along unwillingly. They either buy in or they don't. So we separated, we found premises that we could operate from and the business – Gunther Doyle Financial Planning – was up and running. However the more difficult part was unravelling from the current franchisor. They really played hard ball.

They locked me out of having any communication with clients I had created through them. At the very least I wanted to give these clients the courtesy of telling them that I was moving on. Finally a joint letter to the clients was signed by both the franchisor and myself, which told the clients we had chosen to go down a different path and that at this point they would be looked after by the franchisor.

The model I was developing was a fee-for-service model and there were some clients whom I knew would be better suited under that model while others would be better under the franchisor's model. I wanted clients to have the opportunity to make a choice between – do they stay with the franchisor or do they come with me? And eventually I was able to get to that point. Of those clients that I made the offer to, all except one actually came across. In fact, a couple of the ones that I suggested should stay with the franchisor came across as well. It was a nerve-racking period for us, but thankfully, we were able to work our way through.

The financial planning licence took a while to gain. It is quite a process. There are certain levels of qualifications you need to have and you need to satisfy certain regulations. For me being a CPA was helpful. Having a university degree was helpful. Our business premises was in Bowen Street, Toowoomba. Again it took a while for the money to start coming in and, thankfully, Felicite was doing her bookkeeping and able to see us through. But I just knew and trusted that I could back myself that we were going to make this work. But there was a period of time, weeks, where we had no money coming in at all because we had to sign those clients back across. And of course, the franchisor dragged their feet on making those transfers, even after we had the client approvals.

Rebuilding the Blocks

At this stage, 1998, Felicite and I bought an eighty-acre farm at Biddeston, about twenty-five minutes west of Toowoomba. Almost twenty years later, we still live there. Before buying this property, Felicite and I had a period of separation. Felicite harboured a lot of anger around the whole rent-a-car business disaster and what it had cost us. We got to a point where we were finding it difficult to communicate and be in a relationship.

So I ended up moving in with my uncle and aunt in Toowoomba for about four months. We had reached that low point in the relationship where I wasn't sure whether it was ever going to come back together again. I know Felicite went through some very, very low spots at the time. Her own health suffered and her bookkeeping business folded. I remember getting a call from my sister-in-law saying that I needed to come and see Felicite because she was not in a good place.

So I went to her and explained that we needed to regroup and work out some way forward. I encouraged her to start working again, as a focus for her, and she ended up getting a job at the Freedom furniture company. That was part of her rebuilding process. She made some great friends at Freedom and her whole demeanour improved. We got back together and we started again and bought the farm.

Looking back at our separation, if I try to rationalise it, I had moved on from the whole rent-a-car business disaster and I had regained most of my confidence – I was actually rebuilding. Whereas for Felicite, she had been the one holding it all together for a long time. She was the one putting on that steely face and working through it. It was only when I started to come out of it all that she could grieve and release those emotions.

But even now, and it's been twenty good years since, if I was to ask Felicite if she still harbours any anger from that time, I think her response would be 'yes'. She hangs on tightly to a lot of that, whereas I am more inclined to let go. As a partner, I certainly have my flaws. There are times when I can be selfish and tend to focus on my own needs rather than hers.

I respect the role that Felicite played and I acknowledge that we would not have come through it in the way that we did without her sacrifices. But I have also evolved to the point where I accept that life goes on. I think these days I am more hard-nosed about not taking on passengers. I hang out with people with whom I can align and grow. I look for mutual respect. And I don't tolerate glass-half-empty people. I am less tolerant of pessimism and I am more objective about cutting myself away from negative environment because it is just not helpful. After what I've been through and learned, I just can't be in that sort of space.

That mentality certainly was a contributing factor to us separating – the fact that I was moving forward and being a lot more positive about the future. Felicite was still living in the past when things were in dire straits, so she struggled with negativity. And I just didn't find that helpful. For me, as difficult as it was, I needed space.

And I am like that with people today as well. I don't hang out with people who are negative. If I am in a group where that sort of conversation is happening, I will close out my mind to what is going on and I don't contribute much to the conversation. In fact, physically, I would prefer to remove myself out of it.

The separation left a scar, though. For a long time Felicite was suspicious about whether 'we' were going to work. The farm was part of the solution because we both have a rural background and that was the grouting that brought us back together. We were able to sort of build stuff together on that farm. But it took a long time, years, to rebuild our relationship.

Something to Ponder

What events can you look back on that seemed like a failure at the time but actually led to success?

Do you recognise success in your life or business that has been a direct outcome of adversity?

Have failures in your life or business contributed to learning for better decisions in the future? If so, then you have not failed. You have learnt, therefore you have succeeded.

A PODIATRIST MEETS A BUSINESS COACH

A Podiatrist Meets a Business Coach

'I can teach anybody how to get what they want out of life. The problem is that I can't find anybody who can tell me what they want.' Mark Twain

'The thirst for objects is the greatest enemy of peace. Desire causes distraction of various sorts . . . the mind will be ever restless and hanker after the objects. When this thirst dies, man enjoys peace.' Sivananda

A Podiatrist – Student or Teacher?

So, it was 2008 and I was at the proverbial crossroads. In a few short years, I had turned a prosperous podiatry practice into one that sat precariously on the precipice of financial ruin. The reality of my situation was that the business crushed me. I was in this position due to my ego and countless dumb decisions. I had made my own bed but I still found a way to blame others as well. I laid blame on my staff, competitors, banks and obviously the economy. Despite this, I still felt a huge amount of responsibility for my staff, so I couldn't walk away from the practice, as much as I wanted too. Before I completely drowned, there were still options, such as letting some staff go. In fact, I could have let everyone go and gone back to just me, a sole practitioner, and I would have survived.

That just wasn't a viable option. That option, to me, meant failure. But when I think back there were some pretty dark times while I was evaluating what I was doing, how I was going and what my true worth was as a person and a businessman. The answers were uncomfortable. But at the time I wasn't thinking clearly. One thing I was sure of, though. I knew I had to meet this business mentor – Greg Gunther. But I was shit scared about doing so and what I might learn. I was scared he would confirm that I was indeed a failure and beyond help. After some reluctance, I finally set up the meeting.

There was a newish coffee shop in Toowoomba called Swish. So I met with Greg there one afternoon. Almost immediately there was a connection between us, and as I sat there talking, the weight fell from my shoulders. For about two and a half hours I talked and Greg listened. I kept thinking, 'Wow, this is great to be able to talk to someone.' Greg listens and makes you feel comfortable. He has a sage-like wisdom about him. As I spoke I could see that he was really hearing me, he understood, he 'got me'. I remember saying to him: 'Do you think you can help me?'

His reply: 'I am sure I can help you.'

To hear that . . . it was unbelievable. I also knew straight up that the help would not come cheaply. Unfortunately, I was not flush with cash at this point. I had an overdraft and already significant weekly financial commitments. I braced myself and asked: 'How much will this cost?'

'$3000,' he replied.

'A year?' I said, both of us laughing.

'No, a month,' Greg said.

I remember just swallowing hard. Wow, that was a lot. Where was I going to find $3000 a month? It was on that note that the meeting ended. Now more than ever I knew I needed help, but now I also knew how much that was going to cost.

Determining Necessities

The catch-22 conundrum played through my mind a thousand times over the next few weeks. I didn't know what to do and it was eventually Greg who broke my mental deadlock. He called and encouraged me and convinced me to I should bite the bullet. My first port of call was my bank, who agreed to extend my overdraft to give me a little bit of breathing space.

Greg and I officially started working together in 2008. That was about nine years ago and there have been many successes as a result of my association with Greg, but for me, what he brings is what he brought to that very first meeting. He listens and he understands. So often in life you feel like nobody really understands and you are too embarrassed to tell people how bad some things are. With Greg I can drop the facade, drop the mask and communicate freely.

In business, it is easy to feel like you are in your own little silo. You don't have anyone else to really talk to. You feel like no one will understand or truly care. Well, I needed to talk. Up until this point I didn't have anyone that I could open up with about what was really going on. I was also embarrassed about how bad things actually were.

When Greg and I had our first meeting I explained that I wanted to create a business where I had financial security and freedom. I wanted to create a business I could one day sell. I wanted to create a business that wasn't dependent on me. I wanted to create a business where I could have a choice around how much I worked and how much I didn't. He told me he could help me achieve that. He explained that by investing $36,000 a year with him ($3000 a month), his aim was to give me a return of five or ten times that to make the investment worthwhile.

Now for $36,000 I could actually hire another fulltime administration person. But I also knew I needed Greg's help. Now, the truth is, if I hadn't engaged Greg, I don't know where I would have ended up. Once I said 'yes' the working relationship started quickly. One of the first things Greg helped me with was creating structure and functionality within my work team. Some basic stuff. For instance, I never had staff meetings. We would just catch up, almost as we passed in a hallway. It was really ad hoc. So, we formalised a meeting structure.

The key foundation stone was functionality. This comes down to looking at the areas of business where you have the 'black', which is your future dollars (e.g. marketing, strategy, training), the 'blue' or the current dollars you are bringing in each day (e.g. treating patients) and then the 'red' – activities that bring in no dollars (e.g. support roles – administration). We looked at the business and said: 'Well, righto, who is working in the no dollars section, who is working in the day-to-day dollars and who is working in the future?' We soon discovered there was little, if any, work happening on future revenue. It was all either blue or red. And I had my hands in everything. That had to change.

Next we worked on the individual roles within the business – who was doing what. I was fearful about how that would be received by the staff and if anyone would be keen to take on added responsibility if required. The outcome surprised me. The staff enjoyed the structured approach.

Create or React – Choice or Victim?

Another concept Greg introduced early on was the relationship between living your life in creation or reaction. He modelled it on a whiteboard, explaining how you can live a life at choice, or you can live a life as a victim. He also talked about how we can communicate, how we can hold each other accountable.

Now we were looking at the culture of the business for the first time – the way we did things at work. This was a new frontier for me. In the background around the same time, my brother Chris was helping me out with some personal development. He introduced me to some of the Tony Robbins material and he took me to one of his events. It was all in alignment.

So I started having more of an awareness around how this kind of material could assist me. I started buying different courses, books, and like the other 95% of people who wouldn't complete the material, I would get enough out of it to realise I had so much more to learn. Greg explained that 'the stuff' that shows up in our lives is really a reflection of us. A lot of the problems I was having with staff and also with the business was a reflection of how I was showing up.

As has always been the case with me, I am a slow learner, slow to mature. But Greg was incredibly patient as he guided me on a path of self-discovery. The change in me was significant – to the extent that, in a good way, Greg and the staff will now talk about the 'old Troy' and the 'new Troy'. The old Troy was a bit more of a firebrand, erratic, irrational and read to blow up at anything. Sadly the staff were terrified of 'old Troy'. It was my way or the highway. I had my failings, and while I wasn't forcing people to do things that I wouldn't do, I did expect staff to be more like me – to do things how I did things.

And I couldn't understand why they sometimes didn't. Greg showed me over time that I don't want to employ people like me because I wouldn't work for me. 'I' would go off and start my own practice. He urged me to consider employing people whom I would help grow and support.

Your People Are Your Business

Greg also taught me to embrace diversity – characteristics in potential staff that I would not normally align with. This was certainly the case with one of the podiatrists I went on to employ. And she was great. She and I have had a love-hate relationship. What I have learnt with her is to be able to have someone around who is totally honest with me, who sees straight through me and who tells me exactly how it is.

It was Greg who highlighted that I needed people like her in my life because they are the ones who will hold the mirror up to me and not just agree with everything I say. So, over time I have learned that when I showed up differently, when I looked after my team differently, everything else would start to change.

I was slowly starting to understand. Yes, you needed the mechanics of the business to be right – your marketing, your systems and your finance. But, you know, that is actually the easy part.

The hardest part of business is showing up yourself, behaving as a leader, thinking as a business person and realising the value of putting the time into a business as opposed to merely trading time for money. Because if you are working in the business all the time – in my case, treating people – you are better off working for someone else. You have no right to be owning a business.

Greg showed me that I had the bones of a really good business. I just needed to start treating it like a business. Where he helped me a lot initially was to convince me that rather than being a podiatrist who happened to own a business, I had to change my mindset to being a business person who happens to be a podiatrist. It took me a long time to get my head around that concept, but Greg was incredibly patient.

I think sometimes I would have preferred he hit me with a stick and put a rocket up my behind to get things moving, but he took me on a longer, far more worthwhile path of self-discovery. He constantly supported me, encouraged me.

So once I changed my mindset, it changed the way I looked at my staff. I now think of them as my team. I talk about them as being my second family and try to show them the same care and love and support I would show my children. It is an absolute privilege to have a team; it is one of the most rewarding aspects of business. When you start thinking like that, everything changes. But it took me a bloody long time to figure that out.

A Coach – Teacher or Student?

The first thing I recall about Troy was he was a guy who felt all the pain of having to be everything in his business. He was a perfectly good podiatrist and a highly recognised one. He had worked at the Commonwealth Games as the podiatrist for some of the Aussie teams at the 2006 Melbourne Games. So he certainly knew his craft. However his pain centred around him being the business. He generated most of the cash flow. Without Troy being hands-on, the revenue would have dropped significantly in his business and it probably would have folded.

I will always remember sitting down with Troy at that first meeting and seeing the pain on his face. I could see the hint of tears welling up in his eyes. It was a difficult conversation for him, to have to open up to somebody – at the time a total stranger – about what he was really going through.

Troy, like a lot of professionals, wants to put across the persona that 'I am very successful' and there is certainly ego driving that. So yes, it was a difficult conversation, one that I have no doubt would not have happened without a mutual connection who was not only a client of mine but also a friend of his.

Troy was one of my first clients in my new business where I used not only what I had learned throughout my career but also in my personal life and growth periods to help him recover.

That first meeting was held in a café in Toowoomba called Swish. It was an afternoon meeting, one that almost didn't happen because there was hesitancy from Troy to meet. No doubt he felt that this was going to be a difficult conversation, and it was probably one he didn't particularly want to have. So there was a bit of waffling in terms of arranging the appointment itself.

One thing I have learned, and I continue to learn, is that the process of re-shaping a business is a team effort. When you are working with somebody, they have to be working with you as well. If it is one-sided, it will not work. So I went to the meeting with an open mind. I do find it difficult to say 'no', but I was prepared to say 'no' to Troy only because there was that initial reluctance on his part. However I felt an obligation to the client who had introduced Troy to at least do the meeting.

When we finally met, we talked for about an hour and a half. When Troy did start to talk, he came into a space where he was prepared to open up. So I let him do that. We talked a lot about what he was feeling, about the business itself – what he felt was going okay, what wasn't going so well, what some of his key struggles were. I remember feeling his pain because one of the advantages of having been in business for yourself is you have experienced most of these same situations too.

Normally I would not have taken Troy on. He was a client whose business was probably in too early a stage for me in terms of where I would normally start to work with somebody. But his passion and his desire to shift connected with me so strongly. I knew my fee was going to be confronting for him. I knew it was going to be a challenge, but if I am going to commit to someone and their business, I don't discount at all. This is what it is.

In fact, what Troy pays me is considerably less than what we charge nowadays. So when I presented him with that fee, I remember the ashen look that came over his face. I could actually see the blood draining from it. He just sat and digested what I had told him.

This happened towards the end of our meeting and he still indicated that he needed to bring me on board. He certainly gave me that undertaking, but my own personal feeling was that 'cash flow would be an issue' and I was unsure if we would proceed with anything. That is how I left the meeting.

Believing in the Client

All of the symptoms in Troy's business I knew I could remedy. Symptomatically it was a business that I could assist. What it wasn't, though, was a business of size enough where my fee wouldn't become an imposition. It was a significant outlay. I could understand Troy being hesitant – if you are going to take somebody on at that cost, you are going to have to be bloody confident that it is going to work.

So for him to make it all work, we needed to actually grow that business. That was going to be some of the initial focus. For me, I was prepared to take Troy on as a client – if he decided to – because there was that immediate connection and I just believed in him. He was at a point where he knew he had to make changes and certainly appeared ready to not only heed my counsel but to step up and act on it.

Of course a situation like this can never be plain sailing on calm waters. It is interesting when you work with young professionals. While they will give you all the verbal signs that they are willing, there is still a large slice of personal pride involved. The one thing I have learned is to know how hard to push.

In the early days working with Troy, I came in fairly hard, which was quite calculated on my part. Initially I always try to measure the levels of pressure and push back, bringing in change. So with Troy, we certainly did go in hard, and I challenged much of his normal thinking. I was met with some early resistance and that gave me the gauge of where I needed to back off and where I needed to push a little bit harder. It was a juggling act because we were looking for early results.

The low-hanging fruit in a lot of businesses is around how they charge. For example in a health business: 'How long is it taking me to see a patient?' and 'Are there ways I can improve that efficiency?' With Troy and his staff, there was no consistency in their approach.

Troy had about fifteen years of experience, while other staff members were relatively new, with only three or four years under their belt, yet they were all charging the same price. I pointed out that Troy was doing all the higher level biomechanical work and others were doing more of the general treatment type work. How could he justify his cost structure? I met a fair bit of resistance from him on that point. But we played with it. He did alter his pricing and that started to deliver results for him.

The fact that I knew nothing about podiatry was irrelevant. I could equate it back to an hourly rate. I explained to Troy that what he was yielding for an hour was similar or less than other people who had less training – certainly not four years of university study as was his case. I told him: 'You have done all this work. You are getting people back on their feet, yet you are earning less than someone with far fewer credentials. How does that feel?' Once I was able to draw the parameters, Troy started to get it.

Troy could easily be equated to a partner in an accountancy practice – a senior partner who would be charging $400/$500 an hour. A doctor seeing several patients an hour should be earning well over $200 an hour. However Troy was charging his services out at barely $100 an hour.

Obviously the concern was that Troy was going to lose clients if he charged more, but he didn't really know that. I also asked what other podiatrists were charging and neither Troy nor his staff knew. Troy's price structure was just what had evolved through the history of the business.

I remember at the time getting the practice manager to find out what other podiatrists were charging, which involved some research, including enlisting a couple of 'mystery shoppers' who were sent to have a treatment with other podiatrists – to see what the treatment was and what the charges were. We quickly established that in a lot of cases we were at or below what a lot of other podiatrists were charging. Immediately that created a confidence around change.

Commit to the Goal

Of course there were early doubts from Troy when we first implemented the various changes. We had several 'discussions'. Many, many a time Troy would tell me in no uncertain terms: 'This is not working. It is too hard. I think I'll just sack everybody and go back to being a sole practitioner.' A couple of those conversations were lengthy. But I remained confident in what we were doing. It was my role to remind him about what we discussed. What did he really want?

That is always the anchor, to go back to your goals and then test how strongly you desire those goals. Because if there is not a total bond to achieving those outcomes, then you are building on sand. I always take business owners back to what we discussed and challenge them around that. 'Are you really serious? Do you really want that or not? Because if you are going to go back to being a sole practitioner, are you going to achieve those outcomes?'

So we had several of those circular sorts of conversation. I remember one in particular. It was a phone conversation and I was sitting in my car in a car park. It was a long and emotional conversation. Troy was getting back to a fairly deep level of emotion – similar to that first meeting. He was asking me, and himself, whether anything had been achieved thus far out of this whole process. He was really challenging both of us.

Was it working? Of course, I must admit, on occasions when I have those conversations, I go back and think: 'Well, okay we have done this and this and this . . . and this is where we are at. You know, *is* it actually working?' So the concerns are not one-sided. But again I reminded Troy that this is the journey we were on and if you look at it closely, the human tendency is always to look at the negatives and ignore the positives.

In that particular conversation, we did have some positives. We had seen some results coming through from the pricing changes we had made.

We had seen some people stepping up because we were getting the right people in the right roles. They were taking responsibility and they were taking a load off Troy. We had podiatrists who were starting to align in terms of their practices and they billed appropriately. So there were some bright spots and I was able to remind him that we actually had these positives and it was probably more a question of time, not timing.

The Turning Point

At that time Troy's major concern stemmed from the fact that the profit wasn't where we would have liked it to be. Cash flow was still tight. We were outlaying quite a deal of money investing in the business itself. So the matrix that you would typically look to, particularly around your financials, wasn't necessarily reflecting the amount of hard work that we had all put in. That caused a deal of pain.

The carpark conversation came about three years into our partnership, so Troy's patience was thinning. I could see that we were only a few months away from a big improvement in the bottom line. And that improvement DID happen about three months later. We started to see the bank balance moving north. The weight was lifting off Troy's shoulders and smiles appeared a more frequently on his face.

That was the big breakthrough, the big relief, and it brought us to a point where we could build from there. The journey to that point and the time frame – three years – was pretty typical. These journeys do normally take two to three years. And I mention 'relief' because I buy into all of these engagements as much as the owners and, even though they may not know it, I take most of this personally in terms of the engagement. I get as much thrill in a success as they do. And there are times when I will get goosebumps or even be moved to tears when we achieve something of significance. There is nothing better than seeing a plan come to fruition.

Letting Go

'Old Troy' would berate staff publicly. He wore his heart on his sleeve and if he was having a bad day, then people knew and he wouldn't mind. He wanted people to share in his pain. He also wanted staff to be aware that: 'I am the one wearing all the risk here. I am the one who is paying all the bills. You guys are on Easy Street because you just turn up and get paid every week.' I have no doubt Troy sheltered a hint of resentment towards his staff.

There was a 'them and me' culture at his practice. Alongside this there was almost a split personality. Troy was the business owner and then he was one of the team. On certain days he was the good boss, likeable, joking with his team and be fun to be around. But it depended on whether it was a good day or bad day, and staff members learnt when to stand off.

In that way he was not unlike a lot of business owners. Partly their behaviour comes from the fact that they believe they have to do everything. There is this strong need to control, a need to be across everything, an inability to let go of particular responsibilities. If Troy did allocate tasks, he needed to be involved in the communication loop and be on top of every detail.

So Troy had to be in total control in those early days. To some extent that conveyed a lack of trust in his team. Now if you employ people for a certain role, but still control that role from the top, then people become despondent and move on. That was the case in the early days with Troy. There was many a time when his email box was totally full because every single thing that happened in the business had to come across his desk.

Troy knew he and the business needed to change. But Troy is the sort of person who needs to see the 'why' of something. This characteristic is actually a strength. In his mind: 'If I am going to do this, then I need to understand that I am going to get this reward.' And Troy can be impatient, so if there is not an immediate gratification, sometimes he will revert quite quickly. This happened a number of times.

We would dip our toe in something and if it didn't work instantly, then Troy would return to old patterns. So there was a little bit of iteration involved in those early on years, building his trust levels to the extent where he believed: 'Okay, I can let go of that now. I don't need to be involved.' That trust in the process took a while. It wasn't easy. However,

I found once we got to a tipping point with Troy and he understood and could see it, then he changed 180 degrees in that area. Now he has totally gone the other way where it is a case of: 'What responsibilities can I get rid of?' He has become a master delegator.

I started with Troy in 2008 and the big turnaround in the business came in 2012, but that crucial trust level came before the turnaround. Earlier, while we were going through our challenges, we had formed a solid personal relationship. The confidence and things we discussed were beyond what you would consider to be just the business. So the fact that he felt he could even have those conversations with me gave me the confidence to say: 'Okay, we have built a really good foundation here. From here on, things will only go up.'

It All Starts with You

With Troy, as with all clients of this type, it is impossible to address business concerns without also having a discussion about that person's private life. A lot of the conversations will invariably involve a personal element. The reason I am comfortable going there is that although it is a successful business we are trying to create, without the personal contribution and commitment, I know that success will not be realised.

So it starts with the person. The business is merely a reflection of the owner. If that business is not what they want it to be, then they are the ones who have to make the shifts. And that is where I need to put a lot of my effort, helping them see for themselves that: 'If you are doing this, what is that going to create? How is that going to show up in your business if you continue that?'

That is strategically the pattern of my conversations, getting the business owner to a point of realisation. A lot of this is highly personal. The business issues may stem from a relationship problem. Maybe there is an alcohol problem. Troy openly talks about a heavy reliance on alcohol and smoking. They were his escape. I confronted him with some of that in an indirect way. 'How is that actually helping?' I'd ask. 'Is that actually solving the issue for you? Is there another way we could deal with this?'

And he has shifted considerably on those issues as his own self-confidence grew.

When I first met Troy in 2008, his personal life was a mess. He was suffering the emotional overhang of a long-time relationship that had dissolved. He was struggling. In fact I would say the guy presented to me at the coffee shop that day was in a state of depression. He had very low self-esteem, wondering 'Is this all really worth it?' So his personal life and business were both at a low ebb.

There weren't really many bright spots to point to. He was a beaten man when I first met with him. So we could talk about the business as much as we liked and how we could change things, but I could see that until we were able to turn Troy's state of mind around, nothing much else was going to change.

Again, because I had been there through my own personal experiences with a business failure myself, I knew exactly what he was feeling and that the conversations running through his mind would have been all about failure. There would also have been the embarrassment: 'I am portraying success but I am wearing this very good mask that I am putting out to the general public. But beneath that mask is this very frail, fragile person.'

So there was the dilemma. I could see at that first meeting that the initial problem was with Troy and changing his personal situation. But obviously we had just met so I didn't have the trust at a level to broach that area straight up. He certainly conveyed to me the confidence that he wanted to make the shift. He was a broken man, but I got the very strong sense from him in that coffee shop meeting that he wanted to make the changes.

He just needed some help, guidance and someone whom he could lean on, someone who could feel what he was feeling. I empathized with him and was confident I could help guide him out of that very dark place. That is the connection I felt we had at that first meeting. I felt his pain. And for me, this is the beauty of my work. I have a track record of changing businesses and creating business success. And you can always go back to the business because that is the safe ground.

Nobody really wants to confront the personal stuff. So you don't go there first. But almost surreptitiously you are saying to the client: 'Your own behaviour is creating the situation you are in, so what do you need to change?' You can always revert back to talking about the business, but what you are doing is creeping up on all of this personal stuff.

Through the course of time, as you are building trust, you become a little more confrontational with that, and to some extent, be brave when you need to be brave. There were a few occasions where I had to be very brave with Troy and talk about some quite deep issues. But he has been receptive. And I only go there when I know I feel I can.

Of course that is also part of the reason my engagements are always on a month-to-month basis, so we can both opt out. I don't want to ever feel like people are locked into something and personally I don't want to be either. The arrangements I like to have are ones that if I feel like it is not working, or there is something missing, then we can opt out. And that was certainly the case with Troy. We started on a month-to-month basis and that is how it remains today. If he feels there is not value in our relationship, either of us can opt out. Yet here we are, nine years on, and it is still continuing.

180 Degrees

Across the nine years we have worked together, Troy has changed 180 degrees. He is a totally different person today to what he was. He is so much more confident. He is relaxed. He is a leader now, not the micromanager that he needed to be back then. Today he forms trust in people more quickly and they trust him. I think he is a more likeable person.

If you go into his practice now, it is a happy place. People are happy being there and happy working with him. His staff enjoys demonstrating their own initiatives. They feel comfortable being able to do that rather than having to defer to him for everything. The changes for the better are showing up in his personal life too. He has a beautiful wife and family and he has created a wonderful environment around himself.

Everything, and so much more, that he desired but felt he couldn't have when we first started having that conversation in the coffee shop is being realised. There are things happening in his life right now that I don't think he could have imagined possible.

A pivotal moment for me was in the UK in November 2015. Troy and I were in Harrogate for an annual podiatry conference at which Troy gave a presentation. He was talking about his story and I was sitting in the audience of more than 400 who had packed the room. There were people even standing at the door and outside the door listening.

I looked around and they were enraptured by what he was saying. Tears welled in my eyes and I got goosebumps. In fact I still get goosebumps every time I think about that moment and just how far this guy has come. It really is an amazing story. From the broken person I spoke to in a coffee shop in Toowoomba, now to this man who had an entire room of international professionals in awe, talking about his journey and what he had created.

To this day he is certainly my proudest achievement. What he has done is amazing. His business has grown from the point where he was working up to eighty hours a week and pretty much doing everything that was needed to be done in that business, to now where he no longer sees patients or generates any direct revenue for his business.

The business is now operating without him. He has a much more balanced life and pursues his other interests. He is not directly involved with patients and is now also able to work on the business instead of in it.

A lot of business owners may think about cashing in or selling their business at this point. But if you can massage the business into something that is very profitable and take dividends later and have good people in place, then you will be rewarded in different ways for your many years of hard work. You know your business of course, but could others contribute as much as you? If you are comfortable with stepping back, and are prepared to let go more for others to manage it, then you could reap rewards from another capacity with a totally different focus.

Something to Ponder

Has your personal or professional growth been limited (or even non-existent or detrimental to yourself and/or others) because you feel you have no or little support?

What would it take to reach out and ask for the support you need?

Do you know anyone who could provide the support and guidance in all the areas you feel you need?

What can you foresee happening if you don't get that help? Will you be happy with how you are currently doing?

BENEFITS
OF
HINDSIGHT

Benefits of Hindsight

'Let everyone you meet be your teacher. There is no one who has nothing to give you.' Zen saying

'Too many people overvalue what they are not and undervalue what they are.' Malcolm Forbes

A Podiatrist Looks Back

If It Is Meant to Be, It Is Up to Me

Looking back now, there have been a number of key people of influence who have played a major role in my success, both personally and professionally over the past decade. However, Greg would always remind me: 'If it is meant to be, it is up to me.' And as we know, 80% of business is psychology, 20% of it is actually the strategy of what you do. For things to change, I had to change. Once I got this, I started to turn things around.

I was an adult, but I ran my business and personal life like a man-child. Greg became the catalyst that brought structure around both. My brother, Chris, was gently urging me in the direction of self-improvement and then I had Maree as my rock. But I don't think I could have achieved what I did without Greg. Maybe I might have found another way, but Greg played a massive role.

Chris got me started, Greg kept me going and then Maree helped to finish it off. As I said before, I can always see Greg being an integral part of my journey because he is part of the team. He is a mate. And I am still learning, still discovering. I now have a real thirst to always improve. To me, business is a continual journey. It is not about getting from point A to point B and saying: 'Hey, look what I have done!' It is about enjoying the journey and being agile enough and understanding enough to be able to handle whatever pops up. The psychology of the leader is vital to the success of the business.

There was a stage when I used to go to work and just hope things wouldn't go wrong. And when everything was momentarily going really well, I was waiting for things to go wrong. I was living in reaction. Reacting to whatever happened, whether it be positive or negative. I wasn't taking control. With a change of mindset, my approach to problems in my business changed. When problems show up, it is a great opportunity to grow and improve. 'Shit happens', but it is how we respond that defines what sort of leader we are and what sort of business we have.

I now view myself as a problem-solver. So when problems arise, we step back and look at what caused this situation, what can we learn, how can we improve the strategy or the system and look for the opportunity present. The little hiccups in business are natural. The question we ask is, 'What is this trying to tell us?'

As a part of my journey, I have had to reflect on who I am and why do I do what I do. I discovered that I have a predisposition to being a rescuer. Whether it be work colleagues, my wife, children or friends, I get satisfaction in being the one who solves their problem, who rescues them. So I tend to attract people who need help. Invariably they would get into trouble again, and again I would come to the rescue.

But Greg never, ever rescued me. He would always just ask me another question. Sure, he would put an arm around me when I needed it, but he would also let me down into the deep end enough for me to realise that I needed to learn to swim. He kept me grounded and let me learn the lessons.

An example of this was when I was contemplating upgrading my car. I had a BMW X5 and it had served me very well. One day it was in being serviced and one of the salesmen decided to show me some of the new models while I was waiting. Before I knew it, I had a quote in my hand detailing that I could drive away in a brand new X5 for $100 less a month than what I was paying now. Great deal, right? I was sold but decided that I would contemplate it over the weekend. On my way home, I gave Greg a call. I was rather excited with the prospect of my new car and the idea of 'saving' one hundred bucks a month.

The fantasy balloon I had in my head quickly deflated. In my mind I was going to save $100 a month and have a beautiful, shiny new toy. But Greg, the realist, simply pointed out that I was just three months from saving myself $1700 a month! You see in three months, I would have paid out my lease and I would be making no repayments. Purchasing this new car was signing myself up for another five years of $1600 per month. Greg's wife, Felicite, was in his car while we were having this discussion and she loves telling the story of how she could almost hear my tears hitting the steering wheel. I had hopped on the phone so excited and Greg had taken all the wind out of my sails.

I hung up and thought: 'You prick!' But to his credit, he has probably saved me at least $100k. He has helped me out so many times with similar issues, many of these not related directly to the business.

Greg has also helped me break through my glass ceiling. He challenged me on what I thought was possible When we were first working together, he would ask me where I wanted to end up. What did I want to do? I didn't really know. He asked if I ever wanted to stop treating. I said, 'No, I will never stop treating because I am really good at it and I love it.' He just smiled and said: 'Okay, we will see.' I stopped treating patients just over three years ago and have never looked back.

There were many times along the way that I would get impatient with the pace at which change was occurring. For all of my hard work, I was often frustrated with rewards that I was witnessing. There were many occasions where I would say to Greg: 'Look, we are doing all these things, but I still don't have the money. Where is the money?'

His reply: 'You have got to weigh up, are we in a revenue model or are we in an asset model?' A revenue model is where we would focus on generating cash at the expense of creating an asset that I could one day sell. Now I would have loved more cash, but I was more focussed on building an asset. So I remained patient and we continued to reinvest in the business.

Now patience was never my strong suit and developing it has been part of my long learning curve. Continually I would get frustrated. 'I am not there yet,' I would often complain.

But Greg would calm me down by pointing out all the things we were now doing right. 'Keep doing what you are doing. Follow the process and the results will follow. Trust that you are doing all the right things.' And he was right.

Water the Seeds and Let Go

It is just like that seed that you put in the soil. You water it. You fertilise it. Nothing is happening and then it finally breaks the surface. It starts to sprout but seems to grow so slowly. You keep asking, when will it bear fruit? But, as I have learned, so often people give up when the fruit was just about to appear – it was so close. There have been so many times when I wanted to give up, but Greg helped me stay on track. It is not that he stopped me from throwing the towel in. But he was just there with his hand on my shoulder, calmly telling me that the course we had set was the right one. And to have faith in the process.

Over time I started to see signs emerge that gave me a mental and emotional foothold to keep going. The main indicator for me that the changes we had made were working was our revenue. When Greg and I started working together, my turnover was about $500k a year. The doubts began to dissipate when, after a period of consolidation, we were tracking towards $600k, and then $700k. Next we were on track for $800k and the following year $900k. Suddenly it dawned on me: 'Wow, we are going to get to a million bucks.' And we did.

I remember the first time we cracked a million dollars, I rang Greg with the news. I was excited, elated. To think that when I first bought the practice, the turnover was about $300,000. It really was amazing. Yet the reality was my net profit still wasn't where I wanted it to be. We were still spending too much and the business was still far from as efficient as it could have been. We were still investing heavily in the business. I remember Greg commenting: 'Your first million is always the hardest; the second one comes pretty soon after.' I remember thinking, 'Yeah, right!' Three years later, we hit $2 million.

The difference between a small business and a large business is leverage. And you can't achieve leverage in your business until you start to 'let go' and empower others to do the work. It took me a long time to accept this concept. In the early years I was obsessed with growth. The answer to all of the problems in my business was to grow. That started with opening a part-time practice in a nearby town, Warwick, which I built gradually. I did the same in another small outpost, Gatton, and I started then going to Dalby, about an hour away.

Soon to follow was a number of 'satellite' clinics in Inglewood, Texas, Chinchilla, Goondiwindi and then Kilkivan. These were all small towns within a couple of hours drive of Toowoomba. Things just mushroomed. At the height of this growth, I had my primary site in Toowoomba, a practice at Highfields (a suburb on the outskirts of Toowoomba), the Warwick practice (which eventually graduated to fulltime status) and sixteen other part-time sites.

I had nine podiatrists working for me and I was putting in ridiculous hours (70-80). I was working six days a week. So much for the good old days when I was just coming in four days and having every Friday off. I knew things weren't how they should be. The reality was, I wasn't skilled at running a business still. Greg was on board by now and trying to bring change, but I found that scary. My comfort zone was in treating patients, so I would just treat more and more. The prospect of working on the business rather than in it – letting go of control – challenged me.

Meanwhile my week was chaotic. I was working at the main practice Mondays and Fridays. Tuesdays, Wednesdays and Thursdays, I was the one driving to outlying sites to treat patients. These were rural sites and I couldn't make orthotics there, so these patients would come to Toowoomba on a Saturday morning for me to complete their treatment. So this meant being back in the main office every Saturday from 8am until about 2pm. The trade-off was that I could bill around $500 an hour for the orthotic work on Saturday. So in my mind it worked, but the hours were piling up.

Structure and Accountability

The key focus for us when we first started working together was to structure the business so it was less reliant on me. The cornerstone of this change in direction was functionality. As we reviewed the functionality of the business, we listed all of the roles and responsibilities that needed to be covered in the day-to-day operations. It became obvious that I was in charge of way too many of these roles to be effective and efficient. Greg noted that we were in desperate need of a practice manager, someone to be in control of the running of the practice. This was a significant hire for me and one that forced me to start to let go.

Our first hire for the newly created practice manager position quit on the first day. Not a great start. Apparently the absence of structure in the business and a designated office was enough for her to realise that The Podiatrist was not for her.

So we went to market again and learnt the lesson from the previous miss-hire. I created an 'office' for our soon-to-be-hired new practice manager by being creative with the limited space we had available. We also made sure that we were clear regarding expectations that this was a new role and that it would evolve over the coming years. It wasn't long before we had our first practice manager on board. As soon as she started, I could feel the pressure start to reduce. Her main role was to answer all the day-to-day questions so I could focus on treating and not have be responsible for everything.

The practice manager was a tremendous filter for me. I could focus on being a podiatrist and when we caught up for meetings we could work through whatever issues arose. Early on I instilled the concept, 'Don't come to me with problems; come to me with solutions.' This holds true in our practice today. This encourages people to take the time to consider the options to resolve the problem themselves and by the time it came to me, the solution was generally a simple choice. It encouraged the team to take responsibility for what was happening around them.

As this position quickly grew in importance, it also outgrew the person we had hired, so again change was needed. It was becoming apparent that while our practice manager had done a wonderful job creating space for me and essentially created her own role, she would not be the person to take the business to the next level. Her task management was excellent but her people management was lacking. Ironically as we were searching far and wide for this key person, I suggested to Greg that someone in our administration team, Petrina, who had been with me for a few years, be trialled in the position. She is just a fantastic young lady. A great worker, a really good, solid person and someone who adapt to what is required of her. So Petrina was elevated to practice manager – a role she has now fulfilled extremely well for about five years. Petrina and I have grown and developed together as leaders and I am immensely proud of what she has achieved during this time.

It should be noted that I did learn a few valuable lessons during our time with our first Practice Manager. Most notably, I learned that we owners don't need to be involved in everything that happens in the business, but we do need to be across everything. You see, I started getting used to letting go and as I was still so busy, I didn't pay attention to a couple of things that I really should have. Subsequently, we got locked into a horrific photocopier finance arrangement for five years, we fitted out a new clinic in a way that wasted the opportunity to have three rooms as opposed to two and we fired an administration person we should have kept. These decisions were all a result of me putting too much faith in someone, being too busy and not taking the time to fully consider important decisions. Lessons learnt and we have since rehired the administration person in question.

So with the business operations working well, Greg and I took the time to reconsider our business model. What was the model that would work best? We were still in the phase of having the central practice and a lot of satellites. There were so many moving pieces. It was a lot to manage. I was also concerned that if I were to lose one or two podiatrists over a short period, I would have real problems servicing all of our sites.

What Is the Worst That Can Happen?

Greg would then ask, 'What is the worst thing that could happen?' Well, if I lost a couple of pods (podiatrists), I could close a few sites. If I lost more, I could shut them all and focus on the main site. If I lost everyone, I could still make a very good living as a sole practitioner. And if somehow I lost the practice, I would still have my skill set and I could still go work for someone else. This mindset relieved a lot of the fear I had around the business. It has allowed me to make decisions and have a go.

As a result of my thirst for growth and saying 'yes' to every opportunity, I now had a large, unwieldy business. It was time to consolidate. I had stretched the rubber band about as far as it could go. I knew that while I had all these people moving across the different sites, we were just bleeding money. There were significant expenses for the vehicles, accommodation, non-billing time and room rental. I even had to employ a designated 'remote clinical supervisor' – an administrator who just coordinated all the remote clinics. I had two cars specifically for staff to drive to remote clinics.

Initially there was a reasonable amount of government funding that assisted with the expenses associated with servicing these rural areas, but over the years this slowly started to dry up. Greg always questioned how much money we were actually making from our satellite clinics. It was a really good question and to be honest, I think subconsciously I avoided calculating the truth. Deep down I think I was scared of what this might reveal. Yes, we had created a large business off the back of a lot of diligent but inefficient work. The thought of having to admit that we were too big and would need to shut some sites was not one I really wanted to entertain. It would mean that we would be letting a lot of people down in areas crying out for our service. I would have to admit I had made mistakes and I would probably have to let some of my team go.

I have always had a fear around having to retrench staff. To do this was to fail, in my opinion. I would have been failing them and failing myself. So often I looked at creating work for people by opening other sites, as opposed to letting people go when we didn't really need them. Now I was approaching my worst staff nightmare – I had to rein in the size of my practice, but how to do this without forcing staff out the door? Then two things happened. First, after having a very stable team for a number of years, two of my pods coincidently decided to move on. And second, I built a brand-new, larger practice.

There was no underlying reason for the sudden loss of the long-term staff. It was just the right time and it happened just as I was about to move into the new clinic. For a number of years I had considered developing the original practice situated on Cohoe Street in Toowoomba. I even escalated that situation by buying an adjoining property – which meant I had three blocks at my disposal.

The development process stalled for a while when there was interest by a couple of fast food chains in taking over the site. In fact, one of the companies strung me along for eighteen months before saying 'no'. During this time, I even looked at other sites to rent because we needed more space. I also had other health practitioners who wanted to move into a site with me. After the frustration associated with the fast food companies, I decided to bite the bullet and develop my own site. In January 2015, the new premises was officially opened and we went from the tiny little clinic of four rooms to one that had fourteen treatment rooms.

The physical change was amazing, but what was even more significant was the cultural change. Previously, I might have had one or two pods working out of the main practice and then a whole bunch on the road servicing the satellite sites. Now, with the increased room at the new centre and with a few staff leaving, I was able to have the one central practice with just a couple of satellites. It made economic sense as well. When I eventually did drill down into the financials of running the numerous treatment outposts, the findings were not palatable.

The income – about $227,000 annually – seemed comfortable, but then when I listed all the expenses, the bottom line was about $7000 profit a year. It simply was not worth all the time, energy, money and effort. So we went from fourteen sites (we had at one stage been out to nineteen) back to four sites pretty much overnight. We had the new facility as our head office in Toowoomba, another full-time site in Warwick (about forty-five minutes away) and two satellites which we serviced once a week each (less than twenty minutes away).

Fears, Hindsight and Managing Growth

I had feared that closing many of the outlying clinics would cause a considerable drop in revenue, but interestingly there was only a small reduction in revenue and we saw an uplift in our bottom line straightaway. So, with the beauty of hindsight, centralising into a bigger practice and reducing travel time was a decision I should have made years before. What this has taught me is that sometimes when things are scary, you can't just put your head in the sand. It also highlighted the need to know your numbers. If I knew my true numbers, I could have made better decisions a lot earlier than I did. There was an unexpected benefit of our consolidation as well. Once we reduced the amount of travel for the pods, everyone got to spend much more time together and the culture improved immeasurably.

In these situations, business owners often get a bit scared about what they will find if they pull back all the layers. You think to yourself, 'It will be okay; I will just work harder', bill more, keep saying 'yes' to expansion, all the while assuring yourself that as you get bigger and bigger surely the profit will come. No doubt there was a lot of revenue coming in to my old business model and we were really, really busy, but ultimately we weren't as profitable as we should have been for a business that size.

Another key lesson from this period was the importance of slowing down to speed up. As business owners, it is easy to get caught up working *in* the business all of the time. In my business, I would just treat patients as much as possible and do what I had to do to keep the business ticking over with the time I had left. Once I started to prioritise scheduling time to work *on* the business, everything changed. It allowed me to assess our current reality of – where are we going? Are we on track? What do we need to stop doing? What do we need to continue doing and what do I need to start doing? A business will not survive nor thrive unless someone is guiding the business at a strategic level.

Business isn't complicated. We complicate it. We make it really, really hard. If anything, we ought to be trying to simplify everything more and more. Following this line of thinking, if I was brutally honest, I could probably get rid of the two remaining satellite clinics as well, but the reality is we are tracking really well at the moment and we are providing a needed service. We have had our best year ever and there is still so much more we can do.

Stepping Back

When you review Greg's and my journey, you could reasonably ask whether we could have achieved outcomes in less time. The answer is, probably yes. But like every work-in-progress, there are always a number of balls in play. When Greg and I first came together, he was still growing and developing as a coach and a mentor. We also became really good friends. Subsequently, I think Greg probably went a bit easy on me at times, when I probably should have had a rocket placed underneath me. I think I was a bit of a slow learner and set in my ways.

I have no doubt I was a difficult person to change. And sometimes you also need to hear another voice. For me, that happened when I was on my way to the Rugby World Cup in New Zealand in 2011. I travelled with a large group of mates and some new faces. There was this guy who caught my attention. He never stopped smiling and had this relaxed but confident aura around him. I asked about him and was told by a good friend of mine that 'he is like a younger version of Greg – he's a business coach'. Intrigued, I introduced myself to Andrew Roberts (Robbo), and yes, he is a business coach but a totally different personality from Greg's.

Where Greg is reserved, wise, an old soul, 'Robbo' is a ball of energy, really enthusiastic about life and business. I knew straightaway that I was craving this injection of energy. So we started to do some work together. There was no conflict with my relationship with Greg. In fact, over the years, I have been asked many times why I keep Greg on. Haven't we achieved our goals? To a degree, that is the case, but we are now working towards different targets and the conversations we have now are of a much higher level than when we first started working together. In recent times, Greg has restructured and rebranded his business with a partner (Joshna Daya) who works more on a day-to-day basis with my business. Greg is still of enormous value to me and the business. He has been almost like a security blanket. We have been through so much together and he is always just a phone call away.

Greg wasn't threatened by my work with Robbo. He knew I needed something else as well. Look, for a while when I competed in triathlon, I had three coaches, all offering something different. I have always sought to learn and to have people around me as a support. Robbo helped me a lot and it was with Robbo and his business partner, Jonathon Heath, that we created The Podiatry Hive. Robbo brought a very different perspective. He had worked successfully with a couple of my mates' businesses, so I knew his methods brought results . . . and just so much energy. Greg and I are really more yin and yang. We get on famously, but we are opposites. Robbo and I are similar. He helped me make some hard, fast decisions. And whereas I can't see Greg and my work relationship ever ceasing, Robbo and I worked together across a couple of years and that was that, although we still catch up socially.

Robbo was the one who really held me accountable to stop treating. Greg was certainly saying to me that I should 'pull back', reduce my hours treating patients. But he never, ever forced my hand. Robbo's approach was different. One day in early 2013, Robbo asked when I was going to stop treating – I was still on the tools five and a half days in the practice. I told him that I would aim to stop completely by the end of the year.

But in typical Robbo fashion, he said that was too far away. So I made a commitment that I would be 'off the tools' by September 30, 2013. Well, amazing things happen when you actually start planning and make a commitment. My aim to cut back on some of the remote clinics came to fruition, meaning I no longer travelled and a lot of my patients could be seen by some of my other experienced podiatrists. So my five and a half days a week came back to two. Suddenly I had time. Initially it felt great, but after I while I became a bit lost as I did not know what to do with the new-found space in my diary.

No sooner was I back to two days a week when Kylie, a very skilled podiatrist who was known to some of my team from their days together at university, suddenly came onto the scene. Initially she said she was aiming to open up her own practice in Toowoomba, but I suggested that instead of competing with me, why not come and work with me? She agreed and began with us in June 2013.

One of the reservations I had about stopping work was that no one could do things as well as me and I feared that the level of treatment could decline if I stepped away. What would my patients and referrers think? Would they leave? However, the solution had arrived on my doorstep. With Kylie taking my place, we lost nothing in the skill set. So, in June, I stopped treating completely. To think I had actually stopped treating . . . the feeling was surreal. Being a podiatrist defined me at that point. So Kylie started, I stopped and we never looked back.

The opening of the new practice on its original site, on January 2015, at Cohoe Street, Toowoomba, is undoubtedly one my proudest achievements. I am so glad that I was able to stay where I first began as a podiatrist, working under Joyce and Ed. The three blocks that I owned were in an 'L' shape, so the design of the new centre posed some issues. However I sat down with a good mate of mine, Wade Johnston, a builder, and we came up with a design concept that we thought would work.

From there I begged and borrowed for the funding, finalised the design and had built a fantastic medical centre that I am incredibly proud of. We went from four pretty average treatment rooms and five car parks to fourteen treatment rooms and twenty car parks. It is a multidisciplinary site with physiotherapy, massage, exercise physiology, a dietician and a corporate health provider.

The transition to the new centre was very smooth. We retained part of the old practice and were able to continue to work there while the new rooms were being built. We did the changeover across the Christmas break – with all hands on deck, including Greg – and were able to start work in the new rooms while the older section was being refurbished. In all, the centre was shut for just two work days.

I should mention, Greg put a hole in one of the walls during the move. Just as well we were mates.

Recognise WOW Factors

To date there have been many high points in my working life. An absolute highlight was being appointed as a podiatrist for the Australian team at the 2006 Melbourne Commonwealth Games – a fantastic and memorable experience. More recently it is certainly our new facility. It is the culmination of a tremendous amount of blood, sweat, tears and money. I am so very proud of what we have created and when I walk into the new practice, I just think 'Wow!' There is an incredible amount of satisfaction in the realisation that through a lot of hard work and resilience, with Greg's support and guidance, we have progressed from a business that was looking likely to go under to now turning over a couple of million dollars a year. A highly profitable, saleable asset that is no longer dependant on me.

What I am most proud of, though, is the team and the culture we have created at The Podiatrist. I do what I do to enable me to not only realise my potential but that of my team. To be a part of helping your team grow and develop not just as professionals but as people is incredibly gratifying. It is also fantastic to repay the loyalty and faith of the many patients we have helped over the years. Just recently, I had a patient stop me at reception to say: 'You know, Troy, I used to see to be one of Joyce's patients about twenty years ago when this practice was in the old house. I remember seeing you when you first started. To come in here and see what you have built now is absolutely amazing. You should be very proud of yourself.' To get feedback like that is amazing and humbling but it also reinforces why we do what we do.

Getting the Right Help from the Right People

A colleague posed the following question at a recent Podiatry Hive event, 'With the benefit of hindsight, what would you have done differently?' I wasn't sure where to start with this. There are so many things that I would change. However, as I pondered the question, a couple of things immediately sprang to mind.

The number one thing I would change dawned on me. I would engage a coach as soon as possible. You see, I spent four years at university learning how to be a podiatrist, only to graduate and realise how much I still had to learn. Yet I was arrogant enough to think I could just buy a business and figure it out. That was dumb. I would have engaged a coach to teach me and help with all the things I wasn't taught about at uni concerning business. Someone to help me with my blind spots, support me and provide that unbiased opinion that has proven invaluable to me over the years.

Success leaves clues, so you need someone who can identify those clues. When I look for mentors, I want to work someone who has been there and done that. I am not interested in working with someone who is going to teach me things they have never applied themselves. Otherwise I may as well read the same books and go to the same two-day seminars they have.

I look for someone who has experience and success in business. Even better, someone who has experienced hardship in business as well. That is the person who is likely to help you avoid the mistakes that I made. You are also more likely to make a quicker transition from new business owner to successful business owner.

Can't Catch All the Rabbits

The second thing I would have done differently would be place a greater focus on my leadership and its impact on the business. Robbo always used to say to me – 'The fish stinks from the head down.' When there is a problem in a business, it is generally a reflection of the leader. We get what we deserve. This is a good thing, though. If all the problems in the business are my fault, then it means I can fix them too. This realisation was incredibly empowering once I finally got it. When I think about who I was when I was running that business in the first three to five years, it is amazing the business was surviving, let alone doing okay. Once I changed, the business changed.

Following on from this, I would have also valued the importance of culture on the success of a business. Again, the culture is an extension of the leader. When you see a business with a lousy culture, I will show you a lousy leader. The best strategic plan and the sharpest marketing plan in the world will amount to nothing if the culture stinks. As leaders, we can't force or control culture, all we can do is inspire it. I have been aware of this for a while, yet it is only in the last twelve to eighteen months that I have finally GOT IT! Culture is now one of my primary focusses in every twelve-month and ninety-day plan. The change in our practice as a result has been nothing short of astounding.

Finally, I would have prioritised being a business owner earlier. For many years, I was a podiatrist who happened to own a business. Being the best podiatrist I could be was my priority. The business was a secondary consideration. This sounds like the right thing to do, but when the business struggled, my ability to serve my patients as a podiatrist also suffered. It was impossible for me to function at the highest level clinically when I was battling burn out, incredible amounts of stress and guilt. How could I possibly be doing my best for my patients when I was suffering with what was, upon reflection, depression? Things changed when I realised I was a business owner who happened to be a podiatrist.

You see, if you try and catch all the rabbits, you end up with none. It is the same with a business. You can't do everything. There are three main roles in a podiatry practice. The artist or the podiatrist, the operator who runs the day-to-day business and then the entrepreneur who is in charge of the growth and strategic direction of the business. We can't do all three effectively. We need to choose. If you want to be the artist and focus on being the podiatrist, then we need someone to cover the other two roles.

When I was battling, I was the podiatrist who also did operations with little or no input into the strategic direction of the business. I should have engaged someone such as a coach and a practice manager a lot earlier than I did. It comes back to figuring out what you love doing and what is your highest and best use. Over time I gravitated towards the role of the entrepreneur and I haven't looked back. I enjoyed my time as a podiatrist, but what I am doing now is my true calling. What's yours?

A Coach Looks Back

The new business – Gunther Doyle Financial Planning – was quite successful, almost from the day we opened the doors in 1998. We were fortunate because the client base I had was a solid one and we were able to renegotiate the fees. During my financial planning franchise days, I was one of the pioneers of fee-for-service. A lot of traditional financial planning back then was done on a commission basis. That model was driven towards bringing on new clients and investing new money. That is where you made your money.

Value Your Own Uniqueness

A lot of guys were doing big dollars back then, which from my commercial background I remember feeling quite uncomfortable about. To me it just wasn't commensurate to where the real value was being delivered to our clients. So I pioneered fee-for-service back in the mid-1990s. I even did a presentation at one of the franchisor conferences about it because there was a bit of interest around it then. But all I achieved was creating distance between myself and the managing director of the franchisor. Obviously I was going against their business model and he was uncomfortable about it.

So when Geoff and I started our own practice, I was able to go back to each of those individual clients and renegotiate their fee structures. That gave us an uplift in terms of what we were physically earning and that underpinned the cash flow and the profitability of the business.

How? 'Standard' financial planning practice back then earned money from trail and investment commissions that were paid by the companies who managed our clients' investments. We decided to try something different and went to a new flat fee model. We categorised our clients according to the level of investment our clients had with us. The higher the value of the total investment portfolio, the higher the service level we provided, and the higher the flat fee paid by each client per month. This fee replaced the commission model previously charged to clients. Each category level was provided a different level of service. Service levels were categorised as Platinum, Gold, Silver and Bronze.

In the old standard model, we would have received a large upfront commission from placing investments on behalf of new clients plus a small ongoing trail commission. So it was loaded towards placing new investments and the size of each clients' portfolio that governed our income, rather than the ongoing service we were providing them. The uplift came with the new service model from the fact that we were no longer reliant on the initial placement of investments or on getting new clients. The new business model was solely reliant on charging an ongoing fee directly to clients as relevant to their service level.

This new model was very unique back then and a lot of funds wouldn't allow rebating of trails for clients. The lesson for us, and our challenge? We had to value ourselves enough to have the confidence to talk to the clients we already had and to offer them a totally new payment and service strategy – a strategy that was not provided by any of our competitors so clients were not familiar with the model in any way. We had to be brave. Brave enough to value ourselves enough to ask our clients for more fees in most cases. We knew it was all about ongoing service for them, and their highest priority was wanting to know they were okay and their investments and plans were on track, and that we provided the service to make sure that was in place at all times. We also had to demonstrate to them that we couldn't continue to provide the same service level to them that they really needed with the old model.

So we disconnected from that old model as our highest priority wasn't about bringing on new clients anymore. It was about providing a better service to the current ones. This meant the number of clients may have been smaller but we provided far better value for our current clients. The outcome? We held faith in and valued our abilities, our clients and our high level of service, and we did our homework. Then we challenged having to work a standard business model like the rest of the industry and established a very successful income strategy that had never been tried before. Clients loved it and we were happier that our service level was able to be lifted to where it should be, to look after them as they deserved.

Running Too Fast

Geoff hadn't been in business for nearly as long as I had, so as his client base was quite small, his role was one of business development. My role was to largely maintain and support the existing client base and Geoff's role was primarily to bring on new business. A couple of years into the business, there were not a lot of new clients being added, which culminated in me sitting down with Geoff and have a fairly direct conversation about the need for him to be bringing on more work.

Strategically we decided to open an office in Brisbane and try to solicit more work down there. Unfortunately that ended up being a bigger black hole. We sank a lot of money into that office and it drained the business considerably. We had opened a new office and had taken on a new employee to help run it. But the cash flow wasn't up to where it should have been in the beginning to maintain those costs. We couldn't grow it as quickly as we needed to in order to cover the daily running and lead generation costs. While opening up a new office in Brisbane brought us closer to a wealth of potential clients, we simply did not have enough clients in that area.

The outcome was that after investing about twelve months of time and money, we finally accepted it wasn't working. So we closed it. On a positive note, at the same time I had created a reasonably high-profile business in Toowoomba. I had been a finalist in the Financial Planner of the Year (nationally) two years in a row. So, individually, I was doing very well.

Around this time, I was appointed to the National Financial Planning Association Board, a position I held for two terms – four years – from 1998 to 2002. Taking on a role like that was a huge responsibility with a steep learning curve, but it certainly exposed me to a lot of great contacts. I learned an awful lot through that period while representing the financial planning community.

Identifying a Need and Taking Action

So I had a role where I took on responsibilities for the industry. It was also a period when the profession was going through a great deal of regulatory change. One of the major changes was the creation and implementing of the Financial Services Reform Bill. I was involved at that national board level in having input into that bill. It has created a far more professional financial planning industry.

That bill vindicated many of my beliefs surrounding the financial planning sector. I was able to convey those beliefs and they were largely realised through that period of time. Many of us pushed to put some qualifications around what constitutes a financial planner. We lobbied government to have financial planning as a designated profession. Anyone could call themselves a financial planner then, so we were keen for the government to put 'Financial Planner' as a designated profession, which we eventually achieved.

There were real qualifications such as becoming a Certified Financial Planner (CFP) – a global designation that the Financial Planning Association actually bought to Australia. The profession pushed our financial planners to pursue these qualifications and go through the process of education. So as a board we started requiring our own members to progress towards becoming a CFP. And I was one of the very first CFPs in Australia.

I was gaining a robust profile through my work on the National Financial Planning Association Board. It was also an excellent networking opportunity. During my first term (two years) on the board, I became good friends with the outgoing chairman. We started having the occasional late-night conversation about what he was going to do beyond being the chairman. That conversation turned to talk of him joining us as a partner in our firm. This quickly came to fruition and we added another letter to our name – GDG Financial Planning. My new partner was not only a good friend, but he seemed like a fairly natural fit for the firm.

So began an exciting phase. We had ventured into Brisbane. My business partner was working out of the Tamworth office and we had the main office in Toowoomba. So it was a formidable Toowoomba-Tamworth-Brisbane triangle. However after a bright start, the new partnership dissolved – it lasted less than twelve months. My business partner had been dealing with medical issues and it also became evident to us both that we weren't totally aligned with the same direction we were trying to take.

For me, I had to relearn an old lesson. I had recreated history. I had taken on a partner without confirming that the vision suited both of our future goals. From a negative situation, I learned another key positive lesson, and we both dealt with the situation as amicably as possible. Although it created a rift between us for various reasons and contributed to a difficult negotiation, I was able to let him go to follow his own desires. So, after discussing what would be best for us both, we were able to release each other from our partnership. The result – he exited and we were back to Gunther Doyle Financial Planning.

How did it affect me personally? I was disappointed in myself for making the same mistake twice. I hadn't done my homework prior to entering our partnership to ensure our long-term goals and visions were aligned. I made a note for myself for the future – 'Look back on your past experiences and the results of your erroneous actions when making future decisions.' Once again life reminded me that my choices were my own responsibility.

New Beginnings and Exit Strategies

It was now 2002. Business was going okay, and this was about the time that Geoff and I decided to close the office in Brisbane. It just wasn't bringing the return to justify a physical presence there, although we still retained Brisbane clients. Around this time we started getting involved in conversations with a couple of guys who owned financial planning practices in our region. They dreamed of merging a number of successful financial entities into the one large organisation.

I was fairly lukewarm to the whole concept initially. But as conversations continued over a period of about twelve months, we decided, 'Okay there is some good alignment here.' The timing was also good because Geoff and I were getting to a point where we were going to dissolve our partnership. There was no ill-will here, we just wanted different things. I have no doubt Geoff saw the merger situation as an opportunity to cash in and go do something else.

So Gunther Doyle Financial Planning was no more and I was looking at joining up with three other practices in Fortitude Valley, Toowoomba and Brisbane City.

In 2004, the four of us started the new business called 4People. Although there were the four of us, the name highlighted our mission to be there 'For People', to be a genuine help to clients – we had financial services for people, we had insurance for people and so forth. And the business worked well. I was the older, senior partner, and I had the more mature client base. The other partners were more involved in bringing in new business. We moved into new premises in Hume Street, Toowoomba – offices that were purpose-built for us. And we also had an office in Brisbane.

4People was an exciting and successful ride, but three years in – 2007 – I decided to sell out of the practice. There were a number of different reasons, but it came down to the fact that I had made myself redundant. I now had a team around me who were doing a lot of the servicing of my clients and I was at a point where I wasn't really doing a lot of client-facing work. I remember a particular strategic planning meeting where the guys were keen to go through another step up in growth. Because I was the senior partner they wanted me to be more involved in attracting new business.

I had come full circle. I realised I really wasn't up for that. So I had to get honest with the guys and tell them I wasn't prepared to do that. It wasn't a surprise to them; they had guessed that's where I was heading, but it triggered the dissolution of that partnership, which was all very amicable.

One of the reasons it was so amicable was that a lesson I had learned a long time before was to make sure you plan your exit before you enter. Thus the whole dissolution process happened seamlessly. It led a good outcome financially for me, and in terms of friendships, they remained congenial.

Opportunities Present Themselves

The big question was: What do I do now? Financially, Felicite and I were fine. She had left Freedom and started working at Toowoomba Regional Council. But I didn't know what I was going to do. The exit out of 4People happened two years ahead of schedule. I always did know I would be exiting, but I had reached that point far sooner than I'd predicted. So financially I wasn't stressed around having to find something quickly. I just wasn't definite on what I wanted to do next.

I really didn't want to stay in financial planning and because of what I had just stepped out of, I faced certain preclusions geographically around going back into that business. However life has a way of deciding for you. Soon after I left 4People, I received several approaches. A couple in particular interested me. They were from people who were in my business network. And the approach boiled down to: 'While you are sorting yourself out, deciding what to do next, can you come and help us out?'

It was a case of people around me identifying skill sets that I had that I didn't really recognise or put to the fore. I remember asking one of these potential clients: 'What do you want me to do?' The reply was: 'I want you to do for me what you have done for yourself.' Again, I was mystified until this particular businessman said: 'Well, you made yourself redundant in your business. That is what I want for me.'

He was talking about a three-year timeframe. And that is where the next phase started. Many years later, I still haven't put a name on what I do. I mentor. I coach. I business plan. So I don't know what specific label to put on it. I've worn a number of different hats depending on the circumstance. I'm a strategic planner. I'm a mentor and a coach. I'm a mediator. I am whatever is needed.

When I left 4People, my career path forward was fluid and I was happy with that. Financially there were no stresses to find something quickly, but I logically thought I would end up consulting to the financial planning industry in some form. But now that acquaintances from within my business network approached me to take on more of a business mentoring role, I started to seriously consider that as a fulltime option.

The more I went in that direction, the more I found my energy levels increasing. I was also reassured by the fact that the skills I had gained through experiences applied across most industries. In fact my very first significant client was a husband and wife team – owners of a veterinary practice. Although this was totally outside what I thought was my field of expertise, the same business fundamentals applied and I was able to help them a great deal.

At this stage, I recognised that my background would be useful as a company director. So I put myself through the Australian Institute of Company Directors course with a view to upskilling myself and potentially seeking board positions. There I could take a lot of my experience and learning and apply it across industries or at a governance level. The directors' course was extremely beneficial in a number of ways and was the key stepping stone to me being appointed to a number of boards.

One of the first board positions that came along was with Queensland Hockey. My appointment to their board was a deviation for them. Up until then the board had been composed of people heavily involved in hockey at various levels, mostly former players. However there had been a groundswell of thinking from some of their senior management team and a couple of board members to create a higher level of governance and therefore bring on an 'independent'.

Although I am a sports lover, I certainly had never been a hockey player. I was asked along to the AGM because there had to be a nomination process. I was nominated and seconded and then had to present to the AGM. I could certainly sense that my nomination, while not unwelcome, was not 'the norm'. I was a non-hockey player, independent, and that was something quite different for them. Although there were a couple of other nominations, I was duly elected to the board and remained there for a couple of years. This was from 2006-2008.

I was also appointed to other boards. I did not seek these positions for monetary gain. Remuneration only covered your expenses. For me, it was about the experience working in an environment where I was having to provide some governance skills and, in the case of Queensland Hockey for example, trying to help transition that particular board from the operational-type thinking to being more of a governance body and into a more strategic direction.

I stepped down from the hockey role after two years because I was getting quite heavily involved in some of my own ventures. I found the timing and the regularity of meetings were becoming constricting for me. But in those two years we did transition the board thinking to being more strategic rather than operational. I remember at the time a couple of the directors being disappointed that I wasn't seeking re-election, which I guess indicated my input was considered to be of some worth.

At the very least I had broken that glass ceiling, so to speak, for independents to be represented on that board. It was an opportunity for me to apply a lot of my skills in a governance platform. In that environment, particularly where you have a lot of strong-willed people who have robust opinions around how things should be run, it was 'my job' to offer a perspective from a strategic view, a governance level, and to present my views candidly. So it taught me how to present without necessarily taking things too personally because I would often offer a contrary view while elevating the conversation up above the purely operational.

Assisting Others' Growth

Soon after I left Hockey Queensland, I was invited to be the first independent director of the Fitzpatrick's Financial Planning Group. At the time that business was privately owned, predominantly by two people who believed they needed to transition their business by having a level of governance in place. So, I was the person they invited to come in and introduce the board structure, and my role also changed from operations to governance – and again, I was the only independent on the new board.

To this day I am proud of being able to get that board to a point where I was able to hand the reins over to a high-profile and respected leader in the industry, who was, and still is, well known in the financial services industry. The timeframe at Fitzpatrick's was from 2008-2012. I was particularly pleased with my performance there because not only did I achieve the allotted goals, but my role required a real test of my skill set, and no doubt added to that set as well.

I was there to help transition that business, create a structure and inject more discipline into the whole operation. It required me to don the teacher's hat to instil the required governance and business practices. I worked closely with one of the owners as his role changed to CEO, requiring him – under the new structure – to report to a board.

There also needed to be a significant culture shift. This was all achieved in the three years I was there and I felt confident that I was able to move on after successfully handing my role over to a high-profile person, who to this day is still on that board as a chairman.

Other than my board positions, I also have sat, and still sit, on a number of advisory boards. These boards are set up to provide direction and support to the owners of the business and bring a level of accountability. So, for all intents and purposes, an advisory board operates like a governing board, but it is not a formal appointment as such. So you don't have the responsibilities or the liabilities of being a director of the company. Over the years I have been on more than half a dozen advisory boards.

Identifying Value Propositions

This was a transitional period for me. Since having left 4People, I was still forming my value proposition – where is it that I can bring most value? The board positions were teaching me, perhaps subconsciously, where I was able to add the most value. I was finding my niche, transitioning businesses from, metaphorically speaking, kitchen table to boardroom. Most people in small business don't have a business at all; they are the business. It is centred very much around them. Without them, there is no functional business at all.

So where I bring value to these people is we create the business and take the owner out of the equation. We start by identifying what is wrong with the business and then begin the process of fixing those things. So typically, over a two- to three-year period, we transition what was a business run by the owner to an owner who actually owns a business.

So gradually I formed the view that a lot of people were in this situation where they were stuck in their business. As I started to head in the direction of assisting this type of businessperson, one of my first clients, and someone who is still with me today, was Troy. He came along about two years after I had left 4People and was referred to me by another client I was working with at the time.

So my future was beginning once again. As I was helping Troy with his own journey, I also became even more aware of my own strengths and capabilities. Ironically, I was also realising even more that my own failures could largely contribute to others' successes, and mine. Yet another lesson learned for myself while moving forward.

Something to Ponder

What benefit have you received from hindsight in some area of your life or business?

What valuable learning can you draw from hindsight that will benefit you now or in the future?

What can you think of that gave you a WOW factor in some area of your life? Have you forgotten how it positively impacted your life or business?

What could you do now, right now, that will provide you with a WOW factor now or in the future?

NOW AND
THE FUTURE

Now and the Future

'What we do for us dies with us. What we do for others and the world remains and is immortal.' Albert Pine

'The teacher who is indeed wise does not seek you to enter the house of his wisdom but rather leads you to the threshold of your mind.'
Kahlil Gibran

A Coach Appraises a Podiatrist

So, how have things changed across the past decade? When I started working with Troy, his business turnover was a bit shy of $500,000. It barely made a profit. Troy had a little bit of debt as he had borrowed the money to purchase the premises for his practice. But if you factored in a commercial wage for Troy, the business wasn't making a profit at all. He was drawing what he could from the business, what the cash flow would allow. But it wasn't a commercial wage.

In fact the employees back then were earning more than he was, particularly his professional staff. So that in itself breeds a level of resentment from an owner. This situation is not unusual. A lot of owners are in that position where some of their staff are earning more than they are, but the owner bears all the risk of having a business and running it. Now Troy's practice turns over north of $2.1 million. The profit, even after Troy's wage, is up around the 20% mark.

The business is in a very healthy position. Troy doesn't practise these days. He stopped seeing patients about three years ago. His role now is leading the business and driving the direction of that business – 100% of his time now is devoted to that. He runs a business. He is now a business owner and that has provided him with the ability to explore other personal interests, business and personal.

He can devote a satisfactory amount of time now to his family when he chooses to. He has a young son whom he now gets to spend time with. There is a smile on his face whenever he talks about little Mack. Also, together we are pursuing another interest – The Podiatry Hive, where we are taking what we have learned out of Troy's journey and the transition of his business from what it was to what it is and using that to help other podiatrists, owners in their practices, to make a similar transition for themselves.

Managing Expansion

The physical changes at Troy's practice have also been dramatic across this same period. In 2009 Troy had a couple of podiatrists working with him. That number grew. It topped out at nine podiatrists at one point when he was servicing nineteen different sites. Of those, Warwick and Toowoomba were the only full-time practices and the others were just visiting surgeries. However these smaller surgeries involved quite a deal of travel for the visiting podiatrist.

For example, one of the satellites, Goondiwindi, is about a three-hour drive from Toowoomba. Strategically, the concept was to use the outer visiting surgeries as feeders for the main business in Toowoomba. But through the course of a short period of time, we realised that unless these outposts had packed schedules, they were unviable.

So we retracted the amount of sites from seventeen back to four – two full-time (Toowoomba and Warwick) and a couple of visiting practices. The two visiting practices are nearby the main practice in Toowoomba. Interestingly, when we retracted, profitability rose, which wasn't a surprise because we were no longer spending a lot of money servicing the satellite surgeries.

But the big surprise was that we didn't see a drop-off in revenue. In fact revenue actually continued to drive upwards, mainly because the podiatrists who were travelling were able to service more patients with next to no time lost to travel. After that restructure, we settled at seven podiatrists, servicing a higher turnover of patients.

Living the Dream

Troy owns the properties where his main practice is situated in Toowoomba, and it always was a dream of Troy's to develop that site. The plan was to remove or demolish some of the existing buildings and redevelop it into a surgery or something else. We parked that idea in the early days because it wasn't a priority. The first priority was to get the business functional and profitable.

But as time went by, there was an opportunity when a McDonald's franchise put a Memorandum of Understanding (MOU) in place where they were going to purchase the site and develop it. That fell through and Troy went back to his original plan – to undertake the development himself and create a whole new surgery. He has achieved this and the development was opened in 2015. Called Range Health, it is a collaborative health model which not only includes Troy's podiatry practice, but also physiotherapy, exercise physiology, massage and nutrition.

The thinking here is that through the course of time, patients will want solutions to a variety of their problems, so let's put them all under one roof. Troy is very, very proud of the practice now. It is a beautiful site. It is fresh and the staff love working out of such a modern facility. Patients love going there as well, not only for the medical services, but also the ease of parking, which was always an issue earlier. It is now a highly professional practice.

A Podiatrist Appraises a Coach

Many years ago, I heard Tony Robbins say something to the effect of: 'You want to get to a stage where people can't tell if you are working or playing.' When I heard that, I thought 'Wow, how fantastic would that be?' Imagine enjoying what you are doing for a living so much that people wouldn't be able to tell if you were working or playing. This is a concept to which I have since aspired. Then it dawned on me that this is where I have found myself over the last couple of years. It is common for people say to me: 'Geez, you work hard; you work a lot.' But I say: 'No, I really enjoy what I do. I don't consider it work.' I am in the office some weekends, but I choose to do this. I'm at choice. I don't do anything now that I don't choose to do and don't enjoy. The caveat to that is sometimes while I am 'enjoying work', it can be at the expense of being with my family. I am still working hard to get that balance right.

We Don't Know What We Don't Know

So now I find myself doing things that I would never have dreamt of doing. As part of The Podiatry Hive, I am now training and mentoring podiatrists here in Australia, New Zealand and in the UK. I have to pinch myself that I have this privilege and opportunity. That would never have ever been a possibility if I hadn't started working with Greg and created the capacity to pursue other opportunities. After all, we don't know what we don't know.

You see, there is this thin sliver of what we know, this other little sliver of what we know we don't know, and then there is this massive amount of knowledge we're completely unaware of. Greg opened my mind and my perspective to wholly new ideas. That has been the really exciting part of our journey together.

Greg constantly challenged my 'limiting beliefs', challenged me around my ideas of what's possible. As I mentioned earlier, this is the glass ceiling that most of us construct, often without even realising it. Greg would keep saying: 'What is next? If we are able to achieve what we are doing now, then what?' The first major glass ceiling for me was that I only ever saw myself as a podiatrist, treating patients day-in, day-out. And that was fine. That is all I thought I wanted to do. But as the journey unfolded, I started realising I had different skills, different interests.

So Greg is far more than a business coach for me. It is impossible for this type of mentor's influence to stop as you leave the front door of the practice. His influence pervades my whole life – in a wonderful way. When Greg and I first met in 2008, my business and private life were a complete mess.

In the following nine years, he has not only guided me through to achieving success in business that I would never have dreamed possible, but he has also helped change me into a better person who has far better relationships with all the people who matter in my life.

There was, and still is, one stipulation to our working relationship. It is month by month and if either of us decide we were not getting what we believe we should out of the relationship, then we can opt out. It is a mutual relationship. So, nine years later we are still working together and I am still paying that monthly fee . . . and still paying for lunch!

The Podiatry Hive – A Podiatrist Summarises

As I created capacity for myself to think and explore what is around me, new skills, interests and opportunities not only appeared but were appealing. If I had kept telling myself, 'I am too busy, I don't have time', I would still be 'just' a podiatrist. When I had more time to look around me, I started to consider, 'Maybe this other stuff will be even more enjoyable than being a podiatrist.'

When I went to the 2011 Rugby World Cup in New Zealand, I met Andrew Roberts. Previously, there was no way in the world I would have been able to take that time off. I created that space. So not only had I created an opportunity, that opportunity grew into a whole new direction for my career.

During conversations with Robbo, he asked me: 'What do you really love doing?'

'I love helping other people,' I replied.

'Do you think there are other people you could help in your industry?'

'Absolutely, but many can't afford to work with someone like Greg.'

'Well, what about a more leveraged model?'

Robbo then told me about a vet he worked with that hated what he was doing and just wanted to get out of the profession. Robbo convinced him to sell his vet practice and helped him start a business mentoring group just for veterinarians. This group went on to be one of Australia's biggest vet buying groups and provides education for vets all over the world.

As Robbo was telling me this story, I knew I could do the same in podiatry. So he arranged for me to meet 'the vet', Sam, and it turned out that we had gone to school together at Churchie. Small world! Firstly I asked him about Andrew Roberts and 'Was he legit?' Sam assured me he was. And then I asked him if he thought a similar model to what he was doing with veterinarians would work for podiatrists. Sam said: 'Absolutely!' With that information behind me, I arranged a meeting for Greg and I along with Robbo and his business partner, Jonathon Heath. The four of us agreed this was something that could really help a lot of people.

So it was from that meeting, in June 2013, that the Podiatry Hive was formed. And the funny thing is, Greg and I discussed a similar concept in the early years of us working together. I didn't think it was possible at that time. Now I'm living that dream.

Sharing the Learning

Our mission at The Podiatry Hive is to transform podiatrists into successful business owners. Our vision is to be recognised as the premier provider of business education for podiatrists worldwide. To raise the bar for podiatry globally. It is about helping podiatrists create businesses that serve them, their families, and their patients.

I believe a significant by-product of what we do at The Podiatry Hive will be an increased public profile for the profession. At the moment, I estimate that less than one in two people actually know what a podiatrist does. This is a fantastic opportunity for our profession. Everyone knows what a dentist does and what a physiotherapist does. When podiatrists have businesses that allow them to stop trading time for money, they can then start engaging in education-based marketing. We need to educate our referrers and communities on what a podiatrist does and how they can help every single individual. Subsequently, the demand for podiatry will increase, as will the level of service and care delivered to patients. As demand grows, so will the remuneration and the attractiveness of podiatry as a career path. All boats rise in a rising tide.

I find myself in a unique and fortunate position. While I have the opportunity to educate and support podiatry business owners globally, I still have my own practice at home. I often refer to it as my Petri dish. We trial different strategies and systems in my practice, refine them and then pass on that knowledge and experience to others. It is great to be able to demonstrate the theory in a living, breathing test case. After all, I am eating my own cooking and not getting sick.

Now The Podiatry Hive does not presume to have all the answers. But we do know what works and we leverage the vast experience of our business network bringing experts in business to podiatry. We challenge the norm and we are always searching for a better way. In this world of disruption, there is never a better time to be looking beyond our profession for what is around the corner and helping practice owners be agile enough to adapt to any imminent changes.

The Podiatry Hive – A Coach Summarises

The Podiatry Hive's genesis came via conversations Troy and I would have around 'Okay, if we make a success with my practice, what then? That is not the end game.' The discussions would gravitate towards franchising, licensing and the like, with Troy's brand as the head franchisor. We did some early high-level investigation of that proposition.

However we didn't really get too excited because it was going to involve a lot of capital and complications we weren't ready for in terms of setting up systems, etc. Then Troy went off to New Zealand for the Rugby World Cup in 2011 and ran into a guy who was on that same trip – Andrew Roberts, who, like me, is a business coach.

They spoke about what Troy was doing and Andrew just sowed a seed: 'Have you thought about running online education and webinar-style material?' As soon as he came back, Troy called me and said: 'Mate, I have met this guy and I think we need to meet with him. I don't know what it is but there is something in what he is talking about.'

Educating with Technology

We had that meeting with Andrew soon after Troy returned and the idea blossomed. The first step, and this took me way outside my comfort zone, was to run an education webinar for the podiatry industry here in Queensland. At that stage, Troy was sitting on the Queensland Podiatry Council, so with his connections and the backing of the Queensland Podiatry Association, we went ahead with the webinar, which attracted about a hundred registrations. So there was an appetite and interest.

From that webinar, we generated twenty-three members. But other than the webinar material, we had nothing else in place, not even a name of the entity that these people were members of. We knew we needed to create something quickly – The Podiatry Hive. So we put together a curriculum. That evolved into having different levels of membership.

The Hive quickly grew from just having Queensland members, to a national base and is now international. Members pay a monthly subscription and the service we provide depends on their level of membership. The Hive works closely with state, national and international podiatry associations, produces a volume of material for members and also exhibits at trade shows and presents at conferences across Australia and in the UK. Membership in the Hive is growing across all levels.

All indicators suggest that it will be very successful.

Greg Gunther and Associates/ Your Business Momentum

A key factor to what I do is, I not only look for better ways of achieving outcomes with my clients but also in what I do. Over time I identified a weakness in the implementation of 'execution' with clients. The client and I would identify something that had to be enacted within the business. Executing has been the responsibility of the client, but I've realised that in order to increase success, we needed someone more hands on inside the business itself – someone who works from my side but also with the key people in the client's business to ensure that changes actually take place.

Growth Strategies

So Joshna Daya joined me as a business partner. Joshna worked with me at 4People as our client servicing advisor. That role was to make sure everything we scoped out for our clients in terms of strategy and process was actually delivered upon and the client was given ongoing servicing. A more hands-on role. She has joined me to now work with our businesses to ensure changes are made in the workplace. She is much closer to the teams.

She connects the strategy to the operations. She works closely with the leadership team in each of these businesses, making sure strategies are executed properly. This takes our service deeper inside the businesses and the results have been really pleasing. We've been able to fast-track a lot of our goals for each company. Joshna takes the clients from strategy to action. As a result, my business is now more of a total package.

Recently Joshna became my business partner and we rebranded our business as Your Business Momentum. Our clients have had high success rates so far. However we will only stay in an engagement if it is working. We will always walk away or step out of an engagement if it is not achieving the required results. And when I say that, it will not be because we are not holding up our end of the deal.

But we will walk away if the client displays, over a period of time, a refusal to work with us. Obviously we cannot achieve the desired results in those circumstances. We will always explore every avenue. We won't just cut loose. If we are all trying and the results aren't coming, we will always think: 'Well, okay, what else could we be doing to get a different response?'

As a norm, we work with up to twelve clients one-on-one at any one time. Up until about three years ago before Joshna came along, I was coasting. I merely enjoyed helping people. My business evolved as it needed to evolve. I wasn't necessarily driving it in any particular way; I just enjoyed doing what I loved doing. It was a nice ride and it paid well.

When Joshna came along, that introduced another layer to the business so I needed to put a structure in place. Joshna has been great at helping me build a foundation that has some great structure around it. I can now confidently map out the client's journey for them. We have our whole pricing sorted around the different offerings that we have. In fact we are about to launch a marketing program for the first time. We are seeking to grow the business and are going through a rebranding exercise.

Future Planning

Greg Gunther & Associates has grown into Your Business Momentum. Initially there were four people involved in the business – three of us full-time and one part-time. Joshna and I are the front line; we do all the delivery and then we have our support behind us. As we grow, I think the first appointment we will make will be an implementer who will work alongside Joshna to create more capacity to do the implementing.

I will keep doing what I am doing – being face-to-face with the business owner, getting an understanding of their issues and working on strategies to meet any challenges. I have the capacity to take on much more work at the front end; the problem up until now has been implementing that advice. And now we have the team to make that happen.

Leave a Legacy

As this next phase of my business life grows, I have thought through my positioning. My role right now will transition towards a legacy – me imparting what I know to others. That is my next stage of life. The realisation for that came when Joshna started working with me. Now that I had another person in the business, suddenly I saw that I had mistakenly made the business about myself. It's funny – we teach our clients to create a business that is not about them, but we weren't even practicing that ourselves.

So I began transitioning and the first step was to be able to take myself out of the business equation and that began with me passing my knowledge on to Joshna. She has been an excellent student in that regard and has evolved into a really good business coach, to an extent now where I have every confidence in her delivery.

The beauty of Your Business Momentum is that for the first time I don't have to work on an exit strategy. No doubt my role will change, most likely to being the figurehead, the person who continues to mentor, coach and bring on others. But that role would also have the capacity to retain an interest in the business itself, maybe even to work with some clients. It will be at a point of choice.

It will be me living out purpose in the best possible way. Now that I'm at the point of choice, I can work with my team or choose to work with a client or in The Podiatry Hive. There will be variety and one thing I do know about myself is I get bored easily so I need variety. I need the freedom to move between various options. Freedom to choose is a necessity.

A lot of my life has been in search of a purpose – understanding just what it is that I am here to do. Every corner that I reached, I thought I had found 'it', only to realise that no, actually that's not it. I now feel, particularly in these more recent years, I have purpose. And I am in a position where I can live that.

What is that purpose for me? It is to be able to create more enjoyable lives for small business owners. I'm free to be authentically me – and to get paid for it. Looking back, I had a taste of that in financial planning, but it wasn't enough for me. It was only about the money in the end while maintaining and growing the business and looking after clients the best way I could.

Now I actually get to change peoples' lives while they are working in the business. But my experiences have given me the humility to know that not everyone is ready for a life change. On the other hand, there are clients like Troy. He was ready and asked for the help. Clients like Troy will do the work needed to grow. I am merely the facilitator, the catalyst. But I am only as effective as my student.

So it's a joy to be able to help – and to get paid for doing what I love. There is no better world than that.

SUMMING IT UP

Summing It Up

'The price of greatness is responsibility.' Winston Churchill

'Few will have the greatness to bend history itself but each one of us can work to change a small portion of events, and in the total of all those acts will be written the history of this generation.' Robert F. Kennedy

A Podiatrist Sums Up

As a summary of my business and life's learning up till now, I would like to share some final key messages that will hopefully also help you in your small business, no matter what field it's in, and in your own life. Although some of these learnings may have been referenced throughout our stories so far, I feel it's important to unpack them further. So what did I take away from this whole journey?

BE, DO, HAVE

BE happy now, DO what you want to do, and you will HAVE what you want! If you reverse that order and wait to receive what you want in order to be happy, it will take you a long time to see your dreams come to fruition. If they ever do at all.

Early in our relationship, Greg would constantly talk about BE, DO, HAVE. The problem is most people, myself included, live our lives with these three simple words in reverse: 'Once I HAVE the beautiful wife, the car, the business, dog and the money, then I can DO whatever I want to do and then I am going to BE happy.' But the reality is that thinking will get you nowhere. BE happy now.

Most of the world lives on less than $2 a day. So, BE happy with where you are and then start DOing whatever it is that you want to do and then you can HAVE the things you really think you want to have. Just make sure your happiness isn't contingent on actually having those things. They are nice things, but being happy and being grateful is a choice everyone can make.

Every Problem Has a Solution

Having a great mentor doesn't make you impervious to problems in business. The challenges that I have faced in my business while working with Greg have provided solutions to some of those problems. But even if you have a wise mentoring friend who supports you, you will still have problems. That is the reality of owning a business.

What you need to do is have a mindset and structure in place, so you can take the top off and look for a solution to the problem. I now think – how can I fix this, and how can I stop it from happening again? I am now a problem-solver; that is my major role in my business.

Be a Gladiator!

You have to be a gladiator. You are going to get knocks and bruises. You are going to get knocks that are going to make you question what you are doing. Keep focussed on what you are trying to achieve, why you are trying to do it, and keep moving forward.

That is the benefit of the great mentors and peer groups around you who can help you reset quickly. On your own, you might get sidetracked for a week or a month or six months when you stray from your set purpose. But a mentor will be able to spot that error, hold you accountable and get you back on track.

Be Aware of the Future – Build the Right Team

Businesspeople also need to be remain aware so they can predict what is coming. That's another reason why it's important to not get too busy in your business. If that happens, you won't have time to look around and see what's coming. Until you start to create that space, actually spend an hour or two a week thinking about what you are doing, why you are actually doing it and checking in to see what adjustments you need to make it, it is only a matter of time before you run off the edge of a cliff.

When it comes to hiring other people, our job as the leader is to embrace diversity. Diversity is key. Diversity allows you to have other perspectives and ideas that could very well lead to a better way. I went from the stage of resenting and criticising my staff to looking at them as my team. Now I know it is an absolute blessing and privilege to have people who actually trust you enough to put their careers in your hands. I talk about my team now as being my second family.

We don't need a whole bunch of people who think like we do. Otherwise we'll miss out on new information and ideas. You may think – why don't they think like I do? Why don't they work as hard as I do? Why don't they get it? The reality is – they are not you. They are not the owner or the leader. They are people who need to be led, they need to be inspired, they to know that they are working towards something. And they have valuable insights to offer.

Our job as the leader is to add to their strengths and not to persecute their weaknesses. Respect your team. I used to resent my staff and blame them for a lot. Then I started to realise that the key to business is in relationships. Relationships with your business, relationships with your team. Relationships with your referrers, and your relationships with your community.

It's much like a romantic relationship. When you first start dating, there is nothing either of you can do wrong. You both look for all the great and lovely things. You give them all the time, attention and effort you can, and you only look for the bright spots not the dark spots. But over time, people take off their rose-coloured glasses. You might get married, have a wonderful party and great times; there's lots of kissing and hugging. And then you start to do things you might not have done at the beginning. All of a sudden it might not be a kiss in the morning, it might be just a 'hey', and the relationship slowly disintegrates.

The same thing happens with your staff. It's all exciting at Day One but you have to work like you did with them at the start. Like your wife – you can't just tell her you love her once and think that it's enough to last forever. You can't sit down with your team and create the vision and the values, never repeat those things, and then think they are going to get it. It's all about maintaining communication and nurturing relationships.

In recent days those are the insights I have started to 'get' the most. Your team or your staff, they are sometimes the cause of your greatest frustrations, but they can also be your greatest reward. If I step back now, I see my job as growing and helping my team. Realising their potential. Dealing with a problem or frustration is nothing when you see them grow and see how awesome they can become. When you see someone who finally taps their potential, it's massive.

The Importance of Planning – Why, Why, Why?

It all starts and ends with planning. If you want to achieve business success, you need to have a plan. If you don't have a plan, you won't know where you are going and you certainly won't have clarity around how you are going to get there. It took me a while to get good at planning and realise how important it was.

Without a plan, you're firing an arrow into the air and hoping it hits a target. If you don't plan, there is no way you can achieve what you want. When I first started on my journey, I was obsessed with growth. Grow, grow, grow. When I first started working with Greg, I had this feeling that I was climbing to the top of a ladder – but a ladder to where and for what? Climbing, climbing, climbing. Part of me worried that I was climbing so hard only to one day find myself at the top and realise I had the ladder against the wrong wall. I thought my only solution to problems in my business was to work harder and grow. I didn't really know where I wanted to go.

So we need to get very clear – what is our vision? What is it that we want to achieve? Now, and in five or ten years out. Then, why do we want to do this? Why is this important? Once we were clear on that, then we could say – this is what we are going to be doing in ten years. This is the target in our business, our personal lives, our families, etc.

Quite often we think we want something in our business life, but when we really get down to what it is important, it is that 'I want to be financially secure' or 'I want to be in a position where I am not limited in what I can provide for my family.' It might be 'I want to realise my potential, and when I realise my potential, it will help me help others' – be it my team, my family or the world beyond.

Does this mean I need a practice with fifteen sites turning over ten million dollars to achieve that? No. I can achieve that with far less, so why would I want to overcomplicate that? This is why it's important to have a plan. I went from having over nineteen sites and pared down to four. I would like to get back to just one. That's where I want to be in ten years – to realise my potential. To realise the potential of my family, of my team, and the potential of all my patients. That's what part of my 'why' is.

Now, if that's what you want to achieve in ten years, what does five years look like? Then what about where you want to be in three years? Then what about in twelve months from now? Just recently we reached where we wanted to be in twelve months. Then we considered the next ninety days and started working in ninety-day blocks. Then, to do what we have to do in ninety days, I considered what do I need to do this week. If you know what you need to do this week, then what do you need to do today.

We have set a process up in our business that every year we spend two days off-site to create the plan for the following year. We reflect on the year that's just passed and then reset and create the plan for the next twelve months. From the twelve-month plan, the priorities for the next ninety days are identified. These ninety-day priorities can then be broken up into weekly blocks. So with that weekly plan, we execute what we need to do today. At the end of every ninety days, we have one day off-site where we review that ninety days. We ask what did we do right, what did we do wrong, where we are at, and then we reset accordingly for the next ninety days.

Greg helped me to realise that when I was stressing out all day, every day, I didn't have time to figure out what I really wanted. He kept asking questions. When I said, 'I want to have twenty sites', his question would be, 'Why?' If I said because I wanted more money, he would again ask, 'Why?' Always why, why, why.

It comes right back to BE, DO, HAVE.

When you plan and decide where you want to be in twelve months, for example, then also plan what you want to do in one week. On the Monday of each week, my team and I decide the three key things we want to do this week to move the business forward. Then on Friday we revisit that and ask – How did it go? We check things off and realise, yes, we are moving forward. But also we get the satisfaction and reward of knowing we made progress.

Those who become frustrated are often those who don't have a goal. They don't have clarity around where they are going and why they are going there in the first place. Subsequently, they don't know when they actually have gotten somewhere. 'One day I might have a million dollars in the bank,' they tell themselves, 'a house here and a house there – then I will be happy.'

But they are missing the point. Happiness comes along in the journey. It comes as we expand as individuals and fulfil our potential. As we progress and tick off goals. As we contribute to others in our team and contribute to our community.

How did I get to figure out what I really wanted? It started with actually creating capacity. Creating capacity to actually sit down and think. Think about what I really want and what really makes me happy. The Hive came from actually having the headspace to give it attention. If I was working in my business every day, worrying about how I could pay the bills and do everything else, there was no way I would have had the headspace to create it. I have now reached a stage with my business where people can't tell if I am working or playing. I love what I do.

Be Productive

Have a clear plan each day. There are emails to answer, calls to make and things to do. We need to prioritise the actions that will actually progress us towards our objectives. Otherwise we just get cause in the cycle of 'busyness'. Without a daily plan, we cannot optimise the day. Also, when space opens up as a result of a patient cancellation or something similar, this time is wasted as we have not clearly defined what we want to get done that day. One hour of productive work with focus is better than six hours of unproductive work. When people say, 'I don't have the time', I ask to see their plan and their diary. Then it's easy to see why they 'don't have time'. It starts with scheduling two hours a week to focus ON your business.

Create plans for the week on Sunday, and when you start the week on Monday, you'll have a clearly defined plan of what you are going to achieve. You are not trying to figure it out on the run. So if you have a window of opportunity when someone cancels or reschedules, you can do something productive that will move you forward. At the end of the day, you will be satisfied and feel good about making progress, as opposed to just being the mouse on the wheel. You will be moving forward to what you are wanting to achieve. That is when happiness comes.

Creation vs Reaction

Create, don't react. How often do days just happen to you? You might wake up feeling lousy and tired. So you hit the snooze button and steal an extra ten minutes. Now you are late. You rush out the door, barely acknowledging the kids, and your partner is yelling something at you as you pass. You get every red light on the way and you spill your coffee on your pants. You think to yourself, 'This is not going to be my day.' You storm into work and things only seem to get worse from there. This is a classic example of a day run in reaction.

I prefer to get into creation. This starts with waking up early to begin a Morning Ritual. The Morning Ritual would typically begin with some exercise to get moving and break a sweat. A 'green drink' would follow, while writing in my journal for 5-10 minutes reflecting on how life is going, what is going well, what needs work and what am I grateful now for right now. Next a short meditation to reset myself and the connection with my Why and the plan.

I then identify what my priorities are for the day. This process allows me to set up my day, as opposed to hoping things go well. When I don't start the day with the Morning Ritual, my day just runs to the agenda of others – busy but not productive. The Morning Ritual is my insurance policy for having a great day that moves me towards realising my goals and objectives.

Enjoy the Journey

I am on a journey, so I am always reading. I am always buying courses and going to different events; I am always looking for ways to better myself and grow. Someone once said to me, 'Hell on earth is to meet the man I could have been.' This sent a chill up my spine. I connected with that immediately. It was then that I realised my big WHY is also to realise my own potential. So what IS my own potential? Right now I don't know. But if I am using every day as an opportunity to grow and expand, this will go a long way towards realising my capabilities.

Realising that potential will also allow me the freedom to choose what I want to do and when I want to do it. And it will allow me to leave great a legacy. I'm not talking about getting a plaque or a statue but making a real difference. This starts with my kids and our grandkids. I want them to be better because of the positive influence I have had in their life. Then I want to help the other people around me. It's not just about getting to the end and saying, 'Wow, look what I did!' It's more about enjoying the journey.

Body, Being, Balance, Business

You have your body, your being, your balance, and your business. Your body is your physical health, your being is your mental health, your balance is the balance across your life, and then you have your business.

A lot of people say, 'I have to get my business right and the rest will work out.' But it should be the other way around. The business is an extension of who you are and who you are as a leader. If there is a poor business, I can usually show you a poor leader. And an unsavoury person perhaps. Remember that saying already mentioned in this book – 'Fish stink from the head down'? I was that person. All the problems I had in my business started and ended with me.

And there are the systems. 94% of problems in business are in the systems, not in the people. So often we blame others for what's going on (or not). Instead, work to create a culture in your business where people don't blame, shame or justify. Don't blame people when things go wrong, don't shame people when things go wrong, and never, ever justify why things went wrong. Find out what happened . . . and why it happened.

Ask, 'What can we do to stop it from happening again? What is the current system? Where do we need to tighten the system?'

Yes, of course there will still be people problems, but rectifying the issues in the systems will make it easier for your team to get their jobs done well.

Don't Do It Alone

I can also recommend that you don't do it alone. If you do, it will be a lonely, stressful journey. Anyone I've ever met who has achieved significant success in their life or business did so with a mentor or a coach. Someone who can give them an external, unbiased perspective to help them see what they can't see. Roger Federer and Rafael Nadal are among the best athletes to ever swing a racket, yet they still have coaches. The coach helps them tactically and plays a huge role in their mindset. It's the same in business. It's a mental game. With Greg and I, our conversations often centre on mindset. When the shit hits the fan, he is always there. If I start to wander or if I got knocked down, he's always the one who is there to help me back on course.

There is only one degree between water and steam. And in business, it is sometimes the smallest of changes that have the most significant of results. The coach helps you see the small changes you can make that you otherwise would have missed. I will always have a coach, no matter what I do. Yes, you may be able to get there by yourself and read all the books in the world, but why do it that way? In the end, you'll only have your own perspective to rely on.

What You Don't Know You Don't Know

Consider a pie graph. 20% of the graph is what you know you know about business and life. Then there is another 20% which is what you know you don't know. Finally, there is the 60% which is what you don't know you don't know. Listen to others. I mean really listen. Be open to others' experiences, ideas and perspectives.

Someone may say something to me and I will sometimes think – 'Wow! I have never thought of it like that!' Or 'I had no idea that was possible!' It can just be one little thing that can totally change your life. It could also completely change your business. So it's always about making sure you are expanding yourself, whether it's reading or journaling or just taking time to sit down and think.

Ask questions like:

What is the most important thing I need to do?

What is the most important thing I need to do to move my business forward?

What am I happy about and what am I unhappy about?

What is frustrating me, why is there a frustration, and what can I do about it?

Indecision, Actions and Fears

The cure for fear is action. There is no point sitting around wallowing and stressing about something, so ask yourself again and again – 'What can I do about it?' Start writing down all the options that you have and then do something!

For example if I am fearful about expanding and what might happen, Greg will say to me, 'If you lost a couple of sites, what would you do?' My answer is, 'I would let a couple of sites go.' And what if I lost a podiatrist? Do I still have the skill set to replace him if needed? Yes, of course I do. The point is there are always options. Greg would ask me, 'What are the options?' I would then start to list all the options and feel better. Then I'd explore my options to decide my next steps.

Avoid analysis paralysis. Like Hamlet, it's easy to get caught up in overthinking things. Some people get consumed with the small stuff. For example: 'What colour shall I make my business cards?' As long as you get it started, you can get it right later. Just do something. Once you break the inertia, then you will start to get momentum. Don't get it right, get it started.

Manage Emotion – Get Others' Advice

Emotion is such a massive factor. You can be the most skilled person and have so much experience, but at the end of the day we still have emotion. We are all a result of our environment and upbringing. So something may happen in a situation that sets you off and you have this limbic loop going on where you can't think clearly. You just need someone to ask you a couple of questions so you are able to reset and off you go again.

So it's all about having external mentors and help when you need it. If you keep surrounding yourself with people who keep telling you what you want to hear, you will never be challenged. You need to be stretched. And if you keep doing what you are doing now, nothing is going to change. If you want a different life, you have to do different things, and also think differently. So get people around you who will challenge you. There were certainly times where Greg and I did not agree. There were certainly times where we clashed. But it allowed me to get a different perspective. I needed that. Then we worked through things and moved forward. But I had to be open to a difference of opinion.

What was it that made me get help with Greg way back there in the beginning? I was depressed. I was broken. I had explored all options. I had to get to rock bottom to realise I needed help. And that's why I wrote this book. Let me pay the 'Dumb Tax' for you. Learn from my mistakes and make the needed change before you find yourself in a similar situation. Just like I wouldn't want people to build a house and have it fall to the ground when they could have simply employed a good architect, I hope you will learn from my mistakes and get the help you need.

And you certainly don't have to be mates with these key people. Even though Greg and I are mates, I still have a huge amount of respect for him and his advice. He isn't afraid to tell me exactly what he thinks. And he has called me out a couple of times on issues where I have erred and haven't been able to see the error of my ways.

I get very excited about situations. I get very passionate. Greg is much more level-headed and calm. He rarely gets emotional about an issue. We complement each other in a lot of ways. Being mates has just been a nice bonus along the way. But it is not a prerequisite. For me, I want a coach who has been there and done that. I want someone who really cares – I want to know that to this person, I am not just another client. Greg has shown me time and time again that he really does care. He even spoke at my wedding. He is someone who cares a great deal about me and my family and my team.

Getting too close in business can also be a disadvantage, particularly when there is a degradation of respect. And I have been in that situation. While Greg and I are mates, there is still a formal business side to the relationship and that keeps it healthy.

It's Okay to Not Know Everything

We don't need to know everything and we don't need to do everything. As business owners, though, most of us fall in the trap of needing to know and do it all. This is want holds businesses back and ultimately results in burnout and failure. The difference between a big business and a small business is leverage. You can't have leverage when you won't let go and surround yourself with those 'smarter' and 'better' than you in their area of expertise.

For example, I am not a bookkeeper. Someone better skilled can do it a lot faster and a lot cheaper than I. Yet I did the bookkeeping for years since I thought I was the best person to do it. That was just dumb. As a podiatrist, my highest and best use was in treating patients. So why would I be doing the bookkeeping or answering the phone? My strengths now lie in creating strategy, working with my team, building sales and relationships. As a result, I stopped treating patients in 2013.

I've mentioned already that every person in business should have a mentor, coach or consultant to help them see what they can't see. When I studied podiatry for four years, we didn't study business. We barely did a subject in business training. Why try to be a jack of all trades, master of none?

Then there are partners – husband or wife, who are romantically attached to the outcome. My wife is fantastic support but if there are emotional issues that come up in the business, I don't always share them with her. She will become emotionally attached and she doesn't always have the full business context needed to deal with the matter clearly enough. So I don't need to share every issue with her. She supports me in other ways.

There's that old saying – 'You have to pick your battles.' I might bounce something off Greg who will look objectively and non-emotively at the situation. But Maree is always there for me. I like to come home and spend quality time with my family without rehashing all the events of the day. I just leave the business at the door and focus on them.

I Wish, I Wish, I Wish

My journey so far has also impressed on me the importance of family. I guess I have always known how much I value family, but certainly now it is far more impressed on my psyche. It is part of that 'BE'. You can go off chasing houses and cars and lots of different things, but there is no bigger enjoyment than spending time with your family and friends. And you need to prioritise that.

A colleague said to me recently: 'Don't tell me what your priorities are, show me them. If you look at someone's calendar and it is full of work commitments and nothing for family, then you know what someone's priorities are.' What I do when I plan is I make sure it is not all about business but also includes family and social activities.

There is a classic story of a nurse who used to ask people on their deathbed what their regrets were. They almost always came down to:

I wish I was truer to myself. I wish I hadn't worked so hard. I wish I had allowed myself to be happier. I wish I had spent more time with my family and friends.

I would like to think that when I am at that stage in life, I will have achieved those goals.

Over the past decade, I have changed a great deal as a person. I have to admit I had set the bar low. I think I am a much better person than I was – and I still have plenty of room for improvement. I now have a heightened self-awareness. I can recognise when I am being an idiot. I know when I am off course. When you have that awareness, you have the chance to reset. Having someone like Greg around means you have someone beside you who can appear whenever a situation gets challenging and say: 'Okay, what is this all about? What role have you played in this situation?' And with another perspective, you can quickly make a correction and again head towards your goals.

Three Key Formulas

Through my work with Greg, I now know that if you want to grow and develop, then you have to keep looking for ways to grow and develop. The definition of life is growth. I am always reading and looking for new ideas. The challenge for me now is although I am continually learning, I also have to find time for 'doing'.

The key is finding the right balance and not to be just running off to look at the latest new shiny thing – the newest sales program, the newest systems program, the newest HR program, gym program or diet. It is a case of following some very basic formulas:

We know what works. Do that.

Business isn't complicated. We over-complicate it.

You have to work on your business and not in it.

We often know the formula, but are we following it? If we are not, then we have a mindset problem. This is where a coach can help. Knowing these 'formulas' doesn't mean everything will magically fall into place. Some business disciplines Greg teaches over and over again with me and my staff. Until you are actually doing it, you don't know it. This is where the coach's input is vital.

Help Your Coach Help You

There is no silver bullet. It's doing the right things, the right way, with the right people, at the right time. And we have to be prepared to do the work. No one is here to save me and no one is here to save you. We need to roll up our sleeves, take responsibility and do the work.

If you are in business, you need a coach. Simple. Especially in a professional or podiatry business. And if you get a coach, don't expect them to do the work for you. You still have to do it yourself. And it takes more than money. It takes time. Time and money will amount to nothing without the right attitude and the mindset. You need to be driven and passionate about what you are doing.

You also need to be clear on why are you doing what you are doing to start with. If you don't have a clear 'why', you are going to burn out really quickly. A significant number of health care businesses shut down every year due to burn out. That's because they don't have a clear 'why'.

As I have already mentioned, my 'why' isn't about me at all. It's about helping other people. I love to help other people, especially to help them realise their potential. While I was treating patients, I would be able to help twenty people a day. When I mentor my team of ten doctors, they each help patients, so I am effectively helping 120 or more by mentoring my team. This is also why I created the Podiatry Hive. I can help far more people remotely than I can one-on-one. Once I knew my 'why', it changed how I looked at things.

I now call myself a coach. I go to podiatry practices to audit and assess them in all areas, and provide a blueprint of what they need to do to turn their business around. We identify what is going well, what isn't going so well, and what they need to do to move forward.

It's what I love doing. I am a coach with my podiatrists, my staff, my family and my wife. I help others to realise their potential. That, to me, is what coaching is all about.

Life and Business – WIP

I really enjoy education. As I mentioned earlier, I read a lot. In fact I challenge myself to read at least twenty pages a day. Most books are about 200 pages, so that is a new book every ten days. I enjoy the process – the new information, the flip in perspective, the application, the challenge.

Something I learnt early with Greg, and one of the most important steps in the whole development process, is to enjoy the opportunity to get outside my comfort zone. I used to be limited by my unwillingness to venture outside that comfort zone. Situations such as public speaking would worry me. Now I look at those situations as exciting opportunities. It is all part of enjoying the process – as opposed to only getting so far and then saying: 'Hey, look at me!'

Good business leadership is not just focussed on growing, growing, growing and evolving and evolving. It doesn't hurt to consolidate and just enjoy what you have achieved. But you can't do that at the expense of not looking forward, because nothing stays still in the business world. So although you have your mini-goals – like reading twenty pages a day – there will be days when you just won't do that. Be flexible. And be true to who you are.

For me, about 85% of what I do I enjoy doing. So it is not a challenge. The challenge for me is to rein things in with moderation. I love a red wine; I would love to drink it every night if I could. I love eating chips, but is that going to help me get to where I want to go? I am certainly not suggesting that now I do everything right. The challenge I have in my life is constantly wanting to be better. I have no doubt my headstone is going to have 'WIP' on it: 'Work in Progress'.

So don't beat yourself up when you don't do things. Just reset and decide what it is you really want and move forward in that direction.

Nine Years Later

I still pay Greg every month, nine years after first accepting his help. There is a business commitment there. I respect his time, I respect him as a person and I don't exploit our relationship. I am sure when I was younger and a bit of a man-child, I might have taken advantage of a similar situation. There has to be a mutual respect. As far as his price – $3000 a month – I have never even considered a change in that arrangement. I know his starting price now is much higher. I respect that he hasn't put the price up on me and he probably respects that I have put longevity into the relationship. I certainly get a lot of benefit still from my relationship with Greg.

When you work through relationships, you progress through different levels over time. If it is a good and worthwhile relationship, it will grow and evolve. Greg has added layers to what he offers, including Joshna. As I have said, she works hands-on with my team. I email her every Monday with my 'Three to Thrive' – what are the three things I am going to achieve this week. Then every Friday I send her an email letting her know which goals I accomplished, and if I don't meet my aims, she asks: 'Why the hell not!'

Greg is now very much focussed on the big picture and leaves the details to Joshna. Originally it was up to me to dot the 'i's. But because I am not a detailed person, my progress took longer than it should have. Now I have my practice manager, Petrina, and Greg has Joshna – and both Petrina and Joshna are wonderful at executing. They work together and ensure plans are put into practice and things happen.

One of the first things Greg told me was that you can be taught stuff, but you don't really know it until you are doing it. That's the difference between knowledge and wisdom. And that has been such a 'real' part of my journey. When he first told me this piece of wisdom, I nodded like I understood. I didn't. Now I know that unless you are doing it, you don't really know it.

If I was to engage Greg all those years ago as I am now, we would have had a very different journey. Our journey has been unique to both of us and a journey of self-discovery for us both. We have become great mates over time, and we have even started another business together. Very few coach-student relationships are like the one we are lucky enough to enjoy.

Look Through Your Glass Ceiling

My last message is not the most important of all but it may be the one many of you relate to the most. So many of us have a glass ceiling like mine. But how do we see through it and then push through it? Imagine the feeling you would have of seeing yourself in the future – one where you have stepped up, pushed yourself and gotten out of your comfort zone. That could still be you!

I think of it like indoor heating. If you set it at 20 degrees, when it gets cooler out, it works harder inside. So imagine you have your 'success thermostat' set it at 20 degrees. That's how successful you think you should be. You've set that for what your life should be like, what your body should look like, how much love you should have, what your business should look like, etc.

You can stick with that comfortable 20 degrees setting if that is your limit to reach. You can go lower or higher. But why not set it at 23 degrees and expect more from yourself in all ways, and then do what you need to do to get yourself up there?

Every decision you make next will redefine yourself moving forward! That's the exciting thing!

So . . . where do you want to set YOUR thermostat? And . . . what will it take for you to get there?

'Hell on earth would be to meet the man you could have been.'
Susanna Eskola | Miltto

A Coach Sums Up

When I sit down with new clients and hear their stories, I still get the same welling of emotions as I did with Troy. I've been there. I know exactly how they feel. What I try to bring to them is a hope – hope that there are ways through the tough times. So my counsel always is: 'Okay, if you are prepared to make the shifts, then we can deal with this. There are things we can do to solve it. But you have to be prepared to make those changes.

Because what you have now is what you have created and if we keep doing more of what you are doing now, you are going to get more of the same. So the shift actually has to start with you.'

This initial recommendation from me is usually one of the biggest challenges for owners. It's confronting. Owners have ego and they are usually quite proud of what they have created. For somebody to tell them, 'Now you have to change', it can be difficult to hear. What I look for in that initial sit down with a potential client is to gauge their change readiness – whether they are in a headspace where they are prepared to make the shifts.

Introducing Change and Letting Go

Of course when you enact change, old habits die hard and the fear flags come up when things go wrong: An example was, we had some turnover of support staff initially because of what we were doing. Yes, we were turning on the Bunsen burner and focussing on what we needed in certain positions and, of course, people feel that pressure and if it gets too hot in the kitchen, they leave. It is seldom a case of sitting down with a staff member and asking them to leave. More often than not, if you have real clarity around what is required, the staff members get to choose for themselves and the process that we work on helps them identify that.

With any client, the initial change always starts with the personal shift. The business won't change until the person has. The owners have built the business with their own blood, sweat and tears so it is a reflection, a mirror, of themselves. So if that business is not working, then I have to work on the person to identify the changes that need to be made.

A lot of those changes will be quite personal. It could be in the way they are behaving – the way they are showing up to work. Or it might be how they are projecting themselves in the business. Troy is a good example. Numerous times when we had conversations around things that he wanted done, his fall-back position if things were not done 'his way' was to say: 'Well, I am the boss. I get the right to say whatever I want.'

This occurred at a couple of staff meetings that I attended. I wouldn't say anything publicly, but I would take him aside and ask: 'Mate, so what do you think was the message you were delivering when you talked like that? How do you think your people are actually seeing you?' That started to work with him and while it was confronting, he ended up challenging some of his own thinking and his approach to the people around him. We often laugh today about how there was an 'old Troy' and now there is a 'new Troy'.

Walking the Steps

Identifying quick ways to increase revenue (the low-hanging fruit) is always an initial step. Another is to quickly establish the needed roles in this business and get the right people in those roles. And if we haven't the right people, then what do we need to do about that? The latter is often a difficult conversation for owners because typically people have been in that business for some time and they have formed a level of relationship.

This restructuring is often a difficult process to walk through. What I do, as I did with Troy, is step the business owner through an actual process where we map out what the business needs in terms of roles. Just map what the business needs. Then we start to allocate responsibilities to roles. Then we start to form some level of accountability – what are the outcomes we expect from the person in this role? How will we hold them accountable for meeting those outcomes?

More often than not, you involve the staff members in the process as well, so it is not just the owner doing this. What I find is that people understand if they are on the right bus or not, or if they are in the right seat. Occasionally, people might actually be sitting in the right bus but in the wrong seat. If you put them in another seat, they step up and perform really well. That certainly happened in Troy's practice. We had one person who transitioned into another role and she is still there – after a couple of maternity breaks – and is performing fantastically.

The primary problem with Troy's business was that it was too reliant on him and because it was so reliant on him, there was a reluctance from

Troy to 'let go'. He felt if he didn't see patients, the business would falter. And so this was the endless cycle for him – 'I can't step back because the business will take a dip.' That was my biggest challenge with Troy at the beginning, to uncouple that thinking and for him to be able to prioritise some of the other areas. So, again, you target that lower hanging fruit so you can get a quick, positive success – a quick win that the client can see – then gradually wean them off control.

Establish Clear Direction

Another early focus was to set some clear direction for the business. Get some goals. Troy never had time to think about his own personal goals because the business was totally usurping him. It was all about the business. So I sat down with him and waved the metaphorical magic wand and asked him: 'What ideally would you like to create for yourself if you could?'

We started to paint that picture and identify the hurdles that were in the way of achieving it. Once we started to tunnel down to some specific objectives and immediate timeframes, we were able to then set up the measures to know whether we were tracking in the right direction. The key thing that came out of that process was some real clarity around what needed to be done and by when. And then tracking whether we were moving towards those things.

Managing Transition

When I am confronted with doubt, the questions I always ask are: 'Are we doing all we can? Is there anything we have missed?' Asking those questions is healthy because sometimes there is more that you can do. But more often than not, you have actually been through all the machinations. You have done all the analysis. You have identified what the priorities are and you have started taking action.

So, if you have done all that and you are monitoring and measuring regularly, which we were, then it is just a matter of time. I have been through this process often enough to know . . . if you can put hand over heart to say you have done all of that, you will keep doing it, you will be consistent and disciplined about it, you are reading the dashboard properly and you are being honest with yourself . . . it *will* work.

Through the transition period, my style is not to tell the client they 'must', but to have them come around to seeing its value. I use a lot of open-ended questions designed to have people start to answer in a way that brings realisation. Questioning Troy's thinking allowed him to link him back to why we were doing this: 'Tell me, if you go down this path and you continue this, what is that going to create? So let's explore that.' I would have him verbalise back to me exactly what 'that' is.

I keep asking questions until we get to that point. 'Okay, is *that* what we really want?' If the answer to that question is 'no', then 'what do we want and how do we then go about reaching that?' Then my job is to hold the client accountable. Perhaps the client articulates: 'Well, that is what I really want and this is what I am going to do to step towards that.' That's great, but if I see that person falter, then I have to be there to ask: 'Why did you do that? How is that actually supporting what you said you wanted?' Usually the business owner will realise they have strayed off course and will realign.

While transitioning small businesses will always require discipline in following some tried and true basic formulas, 'stuff' will always come left of field. Mostly you will not know what or when this is going to happen. In Troy's case, we have had our fair share of the unexpected. We have been through the ups and downs – family situations, personal relationships, staff turnover, banks, financing and so on.

So, you must be agile to deal with surprises as they come along and have the resilience to fight to reach your goals. Troy's pattern follows a fairly similar one to a lot of the small businesses I have helped. Most suffer from the same fundamental issues. The order and priority of those issues may change slightly according to the situation, but all of them have one thing in common. You need to be flexible to meet any challenge that comes your way.

The Thread of Gold

What's interesting for me is the thread of gold that has brought me the most satisfaction throughout my entire work life – the ability to be face-to-face with people and to help them. That's the reason why I have stepped away from the directorships these days.

At a board level you are one removed from the direct input and I found myself gravitating back towards the client-facing and partnership work. In fact now that forms more than 90% of what I do. That is where I gain the greatest satisfaction. I also know what I won't do. These days I am a lot more pragmatic about whom I work with, and I won't take on engagements where I feel I am not going to get that Troy-type experience.

I know if the client doesn't get frustrated first, it will be me who gets frustrated and then you have a parting of ways. So I would rather try to recognise that right from the outset, during the coffee shop conversation. These days with new engagements, that's exactly what I do. I sit down and have a coffee shop conversation with the potential client. If the right fit is not there, then I don't proceed.

Goal Setting and Prioritising

From a mentoring perspective, the key messages remain the same. People in Troy's situation actually don't *have* a business. They *are* the business. That is the first realisation. That is also the tipping point. The small businessperson must get to that point of understanding – 'I don't have a business at all. It is a job and I need to create change to actually have a business.'

So once you break through that glass ceiling, then it is a question of 'What is it I am trying to create?' In the corporate world, they talk about 'vision' and similar catch-phrases. In small business, we talk about 'What do we actually want?' What is it, what are our goals? And many of those answers are quite personal. Most people in business don't have time to think about that because they are so busy in their business. In fact many don't even believe they can have their dreams.

The key is to take the time out for goal setting and prioritising. For me, one of the problems of working with small business owners in the early stages is just getting access to them. They gravitate to what they know, which is working in their business. The fear for them is, 'If I don't keep working, things will fall apart'. So in those initial stages of working with people, I try to help them understand the importance of goal setting and prioritising and allocating time for this.

Strategy Shifts Business; Operations Run It

Once we get some clarity around what we are trying to do, then it comes to execution and often business owners are not really good executors. They gravitate to the operational matters. Most of the conversations I have with the owner end up going back to strategy – strategy shifts business; operations run it.

The execution of those strategic initiatives is often one of my big challenges because the client often doesn't prioritise it and, to be honest, much of it falls outside their skill set as well. Executing new systems generally requires you to resolve issues with people, not necessarily the systems themselves, and this could be right outside the owner's comfort zone. Many of the strategies we introduce are new and, again, for people who have been in business for some years, they will not warm to 'new' because it may necessitate extra time they think they don't have.

So, it is all about baby steps initially and targeting any low-hanging fruits – asking how we can get a couple of quick wins. Identifying and then achieving some early successes builds confidence and trust in the process. Then it's a case of: 'We can start to get on to the bigger rocks and even bigger results.'

Different Perspectives, Different Possibilities

Most small businesspeople have pretty closed mindsets. They are focussed on the work immediately in front of them. My job is to foster a growth mindset where they come to realise they can achieve whatever they want. So I ask a lot of questions. The client already has the answers, but they need to open their minds to it. I work across different industries and professions and one of the advantages of this is not necessarily having a deep knowledge, particularly in the early stages anyway, of the business I am involved with.

That allows me to dig and ask questions. I might appear dumb, but it prompts the business owner to respond and start searching. My job is to try to guide them to an outcome or a solution that is going to get them what they need. Sometimes the client does not realise that something fundamental in the business is wrong and that is only unearthed by me asking some 'dumb' questions.

Another positive of me working across a number of industries and professions means that I can bring experience, ideas and methods from one workplace to another. As Troy has mentioned on numerous occasions, because he was focussed on his profession, that was all he knew. But somebody coming in from the outside who has had experience across numerous professions can bring different thoughts, different ways of doing things and ask the right questions at the right time.

The value that I bring to these business relationships – how I earn my dollars – mainly comes from being available to these people when they need me. There are no set hours per week or anything like that. It is just what is required. And the value comes from them knowing that they have a sounding board whenever they need one.

If you were to ask Troy where has he seen the value in this relationship, I have no doubt his reply would be: 'You are just there for me when I need you.' It is also having me connected to the business. I am part of Troy's business. I value the achievements as much as he does so it is important to me that we hit the goals and we get the marks that we need to. So, for me, it is just whatever is required. I have always maintained I will be there 24/7. If you need to talk to me, just call. Nobody abuses that, but I have taken calls from Troy quite late at night.

Having said that, over the first couple of years there wouldn't have been many weeks when Troy and I didn't physically catch up for a meeting, mostly off-site at a coffee shop. We also set up formal structures as well where we would have management meetings once a month when staff members are involved. So there are formalised meetings and also informal catch-ups.

From my experience, you get the most value from the informal meetings because they are unstructured and not just about the business. They are usually quite personal. Business owners usually go through a lot of their own personal challenges as they are transitioning through this period and Troy was no exception.

However in the early days of our relationship, we were able to develop a level of trust with each other where he felt comfortable enough to talk to me about stuff that he probably couldn't talk to many others about, if anybody. He knew whatever we spoke about wouldn't be shouted out aloud around town. It was just between us. Of course that isn't unique to Troy; that is just my professional background. Whenever a client talks to me, it is always in confidence.

A Mentor, A Catalyst

Having a business mentor or coach doesn't mean you have the silver bullet to success. It isn't about your coach providing you the instant recipe to realising your dream, no matter what small business you own, podiatry or otherwise. Even the greatest business plans and the best mentors will not erase every problem a business will face. Owning a business will always have its challenges. That is the nature of business. So being a member of The Podiatry Hive is not akin to saying we have the recipe and all you have to do is set the oven at this temperature, include these ingredients, do this and you will have the perfect business cake. That is not what business is.

Obviously I am proud of what we've achieved. But I am a catalyst and part of a team. The success must involve both parties. I always remind Troy of that because he often acknowledges what we have done together – to which I reply that I'm only as good as the person I am working with.

I have had clients that this hasn't happened for and that is why I do take great pride in Troy. He's lived up to all the potential I saw in him during that first coffee shop conversation. So to see it now coming to fruition for him makes me happy.

Again, I am just a catalyst, but the stronger the connection that I make with people, the better the outcome, and the easier it is for me to come along and buy into exactly what it is that they are trying to do. I take part ownership of that. And I love it.

'Make it a rule never, if possible, to lie down at night without being able to say: I have made one human being at least a little wiser, a little happier or a little better this day.'

Charles Kingsley

'The only devils in the world are those running in our own hearts. That is where the battle should be fought.'

Mahatma Gandhi

'The greatest danger for most of us is not that our aim is too high and we miss it, but that our aim is too low and we reach it.'

Michelangelo

Testimonials

Disarmingly frank and extremely relatable, *Feet First* provides an absorbing case study of business transformation and ultimately, achieving personal success. Illuminated through complementary perspectives, *Feet First* is a very human story that turns road map. The authors' fascinating journey of self-discovery will doubtless educate and inspire public practitioners and small business owners alike to reassess and improve their own situation.

Scott Charlton FCA
Author of *Your Professional Headspace*

Feet First is so much more than a business book. It's a real life journey through failure and success that resonates with so many of us. This inspiring read appeals to all who have always searched for a way to be successful in both business and life. We CAN have it all.

For me personally, it has taught me patience and calmness through life regardless of where we are in our business or personal journey. There will always be a way through the toughest of times and we come out stronger, having grown more than we could have ever imagined.

Joshna Daya
Founder & Director – Your Business Momentum
Former Campaign Office for Nelson Mandela Presidential Campaign

Feet First written by Greg Gunther and Troy Parsons features the transparent journey of two Aussie guys who set out to improve both of their lives through their respective businesses and inadvertently have influenced the podiatry profession on a global scale. When the book first arrived and I saw the title *Feet First* I wondered how it would connect to the story and having read the book it made me realise that the important thing in life is to take that first step bravely overcoming that first initial fear which gives you the courage to take on the next. All podiatrists could most definitely benefit from reading this book. Too many of us can stay absorbed in the past however Greg and Troy's story shows how one can use adversity as a way to move forward.

Doctor Bharti Rajput MBE PhD
Award Winning Podiatrist, Dundee, Scotland

This is the kind of book that sticks with you. Greg and Troy get completely transparent as they share their stories, allowing you to learn from their successes and failures and apply those lessons to your own life. Those changes made an immense difference in their own lives and could do the same for yours.

Lauren Moore
International Editor

Feet First is a really vulnerable look into the world of two amazing entrepreneurs. Troy runs a really successful Podiatry practice and Greg runs a very successful coaching business and both of them run an amazing business together helping health practitioners. For me, the book was real and honest. It shares the highs and the lows on the entrepreneurial journey and imparts you with significant wisdom about leading a life full of adventure and how to run a multimillion dollar business. The book is very unique and brings you on the journey before Troy and Greg meet, to the transformation Greg helped Troy experience running his podiatry practice, to the future of their new mission working together helping other companies experience the same shifts. Having coached business owners for 17 years, this book is refreshing with its honesty, and so impactful of useful tips and ideas to help you succeed not just in business, but also in life.

Andrew Roberts
Author of *What The Hell Are You Chasing?* and Business Mentor